RN

WASHOE COUNTY LIBRARY

3 1235 02994

P9-AFR-064

A gift
the
NDS
Washoe County Library

Expectations of Librarians in the 21st Century

Recent Titles in
The Greenwood Library Management Collection

Managing Business Collections in Libraries
Carolyn A. Sheehy, editor

Introduction to Health Sciences Librarianship: A Management Handbook
Frank R. Kellerman

Library Facility Siting and Location Handbook
Christine M. Koontz

Promoting Preservation Awareness in Libraries: A Sourcebook for Academic,
Public, School, and Special Collections
Jeanne M. Drewes and Julie A. Page, editors

Serials Management in Academic Libraries: A Guide to Issues and Practices
Jean Walter Farrington

Creating the Agile Library: A Management Guide for Librarians
Lorraine J. Haricombe and T. J. Lusher, editors

Young Adults and Public Libraries: A Handbook of Materials and Services
Mary Anne Nichols and C. Allen Nichols, editors

Moving Library Collections: A Management Handbook
Elizabeth Chamberlain Habich

Leadership and Academic Librarians
Terrence F. Mech and Gerard B. McCabe, editors

Planning for a New Generation of Public Library Buildings
Gerard B. McCabe

Leadership and Administration of Successful Archival Programs
Bruce W. Dearstyne, editor

Video Collection Development in Multi-type Libraries: A Handbook,
Second Edition
Gary Handman, editor

Expectations of Librarians in the 21st Century

EDITED BY

Karl Bridges

FOREWORD BY

Leigh Estabrook

THE GREENWOOD LIBRARY MANAGEMENT COLLECTION

Gerard B. McCabe, Series Adviser

GREENWOOD PRESS

Westport, Connecticut • London

Library of Congress Cataloging-in-Publication Data

Expectations of librarians in the 21st century / edited by Karl Bridges; foreword by
Leigh Estabrook.

     p. cm.—(The Greenwood library management collection, ISSN 0894–2986)
    Includes bibliographical references and index.
    ISBN 0–313–32294–5 (alk. paper)
      1. Library science—Vocational guidance. 2. Library science—Vocational
guidance—United States. 3. Librarians—Employment. 4. Librarians—Employment—
United States. 5. College librarians—Employment. 6. College librarians—
Employment—United States. I. Bridges, Karl, 1964– II. Series.
Z682.35 V62 E98 2003
020.23—dc21   2002028438

British Library Cataloguing in Publication Data is available.

Copyright © 2003 by Karl Bridges

All rights reserved. No portion of this book may be
reproduced, by any process or technique, without the
express written consent of the publisher.

Library of Congress Catalog Card Number: 2002028438
ISBN: 0–313–32294–5
ISSN: 0894–2986

First published in 2003

Praeger Publishers, 88 Post Road West, Westport, CT 06881
An imprint of Greenwood Publishing Group, Inc.
www.praeger.com

Printed in the United States of America

The paper used in this book complies with the
Permanent Paper Standard issued by the National
Information Standards Organization (Z39.48–1984).

10 9 8 7 6 5 4 3 2

Contents

Foreword   ix
Leigh Estabrook

Introduction   xiii

1. The Land Grant University Reference Librarian of the 21st Century: Exciting Opportunities and Unprecedented Challenges   1
   Mary Anne Hansen

2. John Henry's Dilemma   7
   Philip Swan

3. Out of the Box   11
   Marie Jones

4. The Curious Librarian   13
   Kenneth A. Smith

5. Of Babies and Bathwater—Hiring Library Staff for the 21st Century   17
   Danelle Hall

6. Going to Town: Interviewing in the Large Urban Public Library   21
   Alison Hopkins

 7. "Stand Back," Said the Elephant, "I'm Going to Sneeze!"   25
    Janice Krueger

 8. The Cooperative Librarian   29
    Jennifer Inglis

 9. Mere Mortals Need Not Apply   33
    Jane Birks and Liz Oesleby

10. We're Looking for a Few Good Catalogers   37
    Bridgette Scott

11. Hiring Academic Reference Librarians in the 21st Century   41
    Mary M. Nofsinger

12. Librarians in the 21st Century   45
    Barbara Lovato-Gassman

13. Needed: Energetic Librarian Willing to Work in Challenging
    Arena!   49
    Jetta Carol Culpepper

14. Wanted—New Creations: Dinosaurs Need Not Apply   53
    Anne A. Salter

15. Librarians: What Supervisors Are Seeking   57
    Kathleen Fleming

16. Librarians and Human Interaction   59
    Ronda Glikin

17. A Business Plan Model of Employment for Librarians   61
    Angela K. Horne

18. Hot Links Are Hot Hires   65
    Virginia E. Young

19. Technology Skills in Libraries of the 21st Century   69
    Sheila Kasperek

20. A Word to Future Academic Librarians   73
    Vickie Kline

21. Preferred Qualification: Ability to Think Conceptually   77
    Melinda Dermody

22. Voices from the 21st Century: Librarians at the University of
    Arizona Library   81
    Carla J. Stoffle, Patricia Morris, and Ninfa Trejo

23. Being a Deep Generalist   85
    Leslie M. Haas

Contents

24. Academic Reference Librarians for the 21st Century   89
    Colleen Boff and Carol Singer

25. "The More Things Change": What Is a Librarian Today?   93
    Cynthia Akers

26. Reference Staff of the Digital Beyond   97
    Beth Avery

27. It Takes a Cyber Librarian   101
    Janet Foster

28. The Academic Library—Not a Lair for Fiery Dragons   105
    Barbara Burd

29. The Academic Librarian of the Future: The View from
    California Lutheran University   109
    Susan Herzog

30. The FAKTs of Life: Being a Small-College Librarian   115
    Molly Flaspohler

31. Why a Good "Sh-h-h" Doesn't Cut It Anymore: Personality
    Characteristics of the 21st-Century Librarian   119
    Maria C. Bagshaw

32. The Future of Librarianship   123
    Felix T. Chu

33. Arrogance: For Obvious Reasons   127
    Shelley Ross

34. Developing Business and Management Skills for the
    21st-Century Academic Librarian   131
    John Riddle

35. The 21st-Century Librarian   135
    David H. Stanley

36. Academic Reference as a Second Career   139
    Cheryl Gunselman

37. Academic Librarians as Caring Knowledge Managers:
    Are We There Yet?   145
    Wendy Tan

38. Electronic Resources Librarians in the 21st Century   149
    Eleanor L. Lomax

39. Competition in the Library   157
    David M. Bynog

Contents

40. Qualities of a 21st-Century Librarian   161
    Necia Parker-Gibson

41. The More Things Change in Academe, the More They Need to
    Stay the Same   167
    Karen Fischer

42. The Joys of Special Librarianship   171
    Ronald N. Bukoff

43. New Librarians in the 21st Century: The Normalization of
    Change   177
    Lorena O'English

44. Electric Luddites: Special Collections Librarians Make the
    Great Leap   183
    Roger C. Adams

45. Selling Instruction: Communicating the Value of the Library in
    the Age of the Internet   187
    Michael J. Rose

46. Militant Segregationists, Control Freaks, and Techno-Believers   191
    Craighton Hippenhammer

47. Metaphor Matters: Imagining the Future of Librarianship and
    the Library   197
    Nancy Kuhl

48. Seeking: Enthusiastic Artists   205
    Randall M. MacDonald and Andrew L. Pearson

49. Before We Look to the Future . . .   209
    Liz Kocevar-Weidinger

50. Teaching Excellence and the Academic Librarian: Paralleling
    the Teaching Faculty's Track   213
    Martha Henn McCormick

51. The Library at the University of Vermont in 1900   219
    Karl Bridges

52. The Most Important Thing They Don't Tell You in
    Library School   225
    Janet T. O'Keefe

53. Technical Services Librarians for the 21st Century:
    What Are We Looking For?   227
    Gwen M. Gregory

    Index   229

Foreword

Leigh Estabrook

What a lovely and refreshing book this is in its eloquence, elegant writing, and succinct directness. The collection of essays provides rich personal insights into the personal and educational qualities professional librarians hope to find in the newest entrants to the field. Although each perspective is unique, these authors, read together, paint a portrait of intelligent, educated, creative, technologically savvy new librarians driven by a shared commitment to assist people in finding and using information effectively.

In recent years the public have begun to understand the field of librarianship in new ways. Those outside the field, when hearing I educate future librarians, will often say, "that field has really changed in recent years" or "it must be really exciting these days to be a librarian." Certainly that is the view of many of the students now entering our profession. Unfortunately, it is not the view of all. In response to the question of why they are applying for admission, too many applicant essays say no more than, "I want to be a librarian because I love books and people." Application essays for a recent ALA scholarship were similarly weak in vision or understanding of the field today. Cheryl Gunselman points out that "useful information about the profession of librarianship needs to be made more visible and more accessible."

But we need to do more than make the profession more visible. Nancy Kuhl, in discussing the metaphors of our profession, notes:

It is difficult to develop a new way of thinking about librarianship because for the time being librarians are often involved in the same kinds of work that they have always done, though perhaps they now do that work in new ways or with new tools (searching a paper index is like searching an online index is like searching. . . .) Librarians entering the field today and in the future must be able to face ambiguity and they must be willing to negotiate the old metaphors of the library and the new, because for at least the time being we will have to do both.

However difficult the task, it must be undertaken. As Anne Salter notes, "The librarian of the 21st century will be the product of what we observe about ourselves now and the critical self-analysis that follows." What then do these essays tell us about the knowledge, skills, and attitude required of new librarians?

KNOWLEDGE

Knowledge of technology is mentioned throughout this book as essential. It is remarkable how many of these essays mention paper jams and the need for librarians to be able to solve simple problems with technology that can hinder their work. Librarians need sufficient knowledge about technology, not only to use it in work, but also to teach it to users. And some libraries seek individuals with programming and other more advanced computer skills. But, as Michael Rose notes, "[new technologies] to be understood not just to assist patrons with their browsing, but also to possibly expand library services. . . . More important than this is the ability to tell the difference between new technology and necessary technology."

Equally important to many of these authors is knowledge about human beings and about human relationships. Librarians need to understand patrons not only in what they say, but also through body language. This means librarians need to know how to listen to their users in order to answer their questions. "Reference librarians who are articulate, persuasive, and use active listening will be most successful in querying customers to determine information needs, particularly if they are friendly and nonjudgmental, ask open-ended questions, and then follow up for customer satisfaction" notes Mary Nofsinger.

A third area of knowledge included in these essays is the importance of librarians being intellectually engaged—or what Kenneth Smith refers to as "active intelligence" so they have professional knowledge and a broad understanding about the world's knowledge. Leslie Haas states it a different way when she talks about the need for a librarian to be a "Deep Generalist." Librarians will also need to be able to share knowledge with other professionals.

These authors mention some different types of professional knowledge sought in new librarians. Those in academic libraries desire new librarians with the ability to conduct research and writing for publication. Many libraries seek applicants with knowledge of collection development. Some specifically ask for knowledge of literature, including various genre. Others note the need for knowledge of cataloging.

Several essays refer to the importance of business knowledge, including the ability to create a business model or a plan for marketing services or business communication. Related knowledge includes knowing how to think strategically and politically and how to develop financial models. The need for librarians who understand how to carry out evaluation was noted in the business and other contexts.

SKILLS

Repeatedly these essays discuss how important it is for new librarians to have teaching skills drawn, if possible, from teacher education or teaching experience. The most important application of these skills is providing education to users, primarily in the area of information literacy; but they may also be used more generally in library use instruction, guiding tours, including an introduction to library resources, and teaching research skills. Several essays mention the emerging area of teaching using distance technologies.

I was struck in reading the essays by the frequency with which the essays mentioned skills that are not discipline specific, but are critical to effective work in rapidly changing organizations—skills like creativity, flexibility, and the ability to work collaboratively. As an educator, I was struck also by the challenge of teaching this type of skill. The content of library and information science education is changing, but so too is pedagogy in order to teach students the skills of working in groups or thinking laterally. Each of our students is able to acquire such skills; but how well they do often seems related to their attitudes toward life, work, and the profession they are entering.

ATTITUDE

Taken as a whole, the authors of this book describe the type of person most of us would love to have as a friend and colleague. They talk of the importance of optimism, enthusiasm, courage, confidence, sense of humor, courage, empathy, sympathy, patience, altruism, and intellectual curiosity. Molly Flaspohler includes the need for "kindness" and tenacity.

Qualities that I suspect are a combination of knowledge, skills, and attitudes that these authors also seek of new librarians are a sense of values and standards, a public service orientation, and above all a commitment to the fundamental value of access to information.

Finally, many of the authors remind our newest librarians of the changes they must face and manage. Qualities they seek include risk taking, adaptability, assertiveness, and a willingness to embrace approaches from outside the library world. Newly hired reference librarians, the authors note, must seriously challenge traditional librarianship values and priorities while weighing new assumptions. Yet they never must lose their passion for the fundamental commitment to unrestricted access to information.

Introduction

As I began working on this book I thought for a long time about how to organize it. I pondered arrangement by various themes such as interviewing, attitudes, etc. I was also taking into consideration various topics for this introduction: the future of librarianship, the role of technology. In the meantime as articles arrived I simply appended them one after another in the order they were received with the idea that I would reorganize them later. Then September 11 happened. After the events of that day and subsequent days I thought there would be a qualitative and quantitative shift in the kinds of submissions I would receive. I fully expected many people to simply drop out and those that did contribute to have a more pessimistic tone.

In fact the exact opposite happened. I actually had people contacting me about making contributions. The articles I received remained positive and upbeat about the future of librarianship. I have left the essays in the order they were received—with the exception of the first, by Mary Anne Hansen, which I placed there because of its merit. The contributors to this book have been gracious and kind, so much so that I decided to let them speak for themselves through the contents of this book rather than try to summarize their thoughts in a page or two—with my taking license to make one comment.

This experience has confirmed for me what I have thought for some time. Being a librarian is many things. It encompasses a wide range of areas: technical skill, interpersonal ability, subject area knowledge. More than that, however, being a librarian represents adoption of a distinct philosophical position. It is, as the Book of Common Prayer says so well, "an outward and visible sign of an inward and spiritual grace." This librarian's grace, stated in brief, values knowledge over ignorance, order over chaos, and helpfulness over rudeness. This isn't to say that every librarian is conscious of this or acts accordingly, but, as the following essays show, these ideals do exist and people do care—which the readers will, perhaps, find either reassuring or inspiring according to their lights.

As I look over my notes I see that I began this project in the springtime—in an era now, seemingly, both as far removed from and as relevant to us as the reign of Diocletian. I complete it in the depths of a New England winter. I hope this book reminds us, like the fat squirrel that is presently sitting on my snowy windowsill considering me, that spring will come again—not perhaps the spring we envisioned, but spring nonetheless. And that will have to be enough.

Karl Bridges

1

The Land Grant University Reference Librarian of the 21st Century

Exciting Opportunities and Unprecedented Challenges

Mary Anne Hansen

Academe in the 21st century will continue to be an evolving world of traditional courses moving to the online format of virtual learning, yet at the same time, the traditional university as a place of higher learning will continue to exist. Though more and more courses and entire programs are being taught virtually, there will continue to be a role in society for traditional modes of learning, especially the university, and in particular, the land grant university, for some time to come. Land grant universities will continue to be hybrid learning environments into the future, offering students a place and a tradition of learning, an important developmental and socialization process as their parents may have experienced, and yet also providing them the opportunity to take some of their course work online. This ever-changing hybrid university environment offers exciting opportunities and sometimes daunting challenges for academic reference librarians at land grant universities. Reference librarians possessing certain key characteristics will be better suited to fulfill both the library's and the university's mission.[1]

Since its inception, outreach has been one of the primary components of the mission of the land grant university. In keeping with this, an essential role of the reference librarian at the land grant university is in the area of outreach to diverse constituencies. Because the state land grant university is the people's university, i.e., it functions to make education and its products accessible to everyone, the constituencies served by the land grant university library include all citizens of the state. Although students and faculty are the primary clientele of the land grant university, and even though extension agents exist to serve many of the information needs of state citizens, all citizens are entitled to services from the library, and hence, librarians, at the land grant university because it is a state public service institution.

In addition to serving the information needs of the campus and citizens, the land grant university librarian should extend outreach to other library professionals in the state, in particular, those in rural settings who have no other professional network to consult for advice, professional development needs, and so forth. In states having tribal colleges that were added to the list of land grant institutions in 1994, land grant university librarians have the additional professional responsibility of serving as leaders and mentors to the library personnel at these tribal college libraries. Often, these tribal colleges are rurally isolated, and the library personnel may have neither the means nor the incentive to seek continuing education and training outside the state or even their vicinities. Thus, the importance of outreach on behalf of the land grant university librarian to these institutions and their staff.[2]

As a professional at an institution whose mission is to serve the needs of the people, the land grant university librarian has a professional obligation to join and to play a leadership role in state professional organizations. The land grant university librarian, by virtue of this leadership role to other library colleagues in the state, has a professional obligation to be involved in regional and national library associations in order to develop professionally and to bring new knowledge and skills back to colleagues at libraries big and small across the state and to pass it on to them through formal workshops and/or informal networking.

As university faculty and as leaders in the profession, particularly among colleagues in the state, land grant university librarians have a professional obligation to contribute to the knowledge in the field through research and creative activities. Such activities include not only doing original research and publishing in professional library journals, but also engaging with other professionals across the curriculum in interdisciplinary activities and publishing and/or presenting research findings and best practices in widely read or largely attended venues. Land grant university librarians can also benefit themselves, their institutions and their constituencies through involvement in grant projects that bring additional funding to shrinking university budgets and extend research and learning into new areas of study.

Other attributes that will contribute to the success of the land grant university reference librarian include enthusiasm, flexibility, empathy, a teamwork orientation, patience and a sense of humor. Reference librarians are unique in their instructional role on campuses. Unlike teaching faculty, reference librarians don't usually teach regular courses; their contact with students is usually sporadic in both one-on-one reference desk or office consultations, and in one- or two-shot instruction sessions for entire classes that come to the library to learn about specific resources for particular assignments. Library faculty instruct in a broader environment, often in tandem with a colleague, depending on the traffic at the reference desk. Because of this broad, team-oriented teaching environment, the successful land grant university librarian will be a contributing member of a collective mission to support the information and program needs of students and faculty. Reference librarians share more common ground in their teaching role with one another than individual teaching faculty in other departments. Thus, more and more university libraries are moving to an organizational structure composed of teams. Effective team involvement necessitates flexibility, patience and empathy for both colleagues and constituencies; a good sense of humor will only ensure continued success and help the librarian to avoid burnout. Additionally, academic reference librarians, in this same team spirit, should be eager and willing to mentor junior colleagues and peers. Mentoring allows the individual to give something back to the profession while strengthening the organization and ultimately the profession.[3]

In their instructional role, academic reference librarians should strive to teach students and other library users to teach themselves. Rather than just telling students where to find answers or providing the needed information itself, reference librarians should guide users to develop information literacy skills so they become skillful and critical consumers of information with a zest for lifelong learning. In taking such an active instructional role, librarians are aiding in the development of active and even reflective learners. Additionally, the academic reference librarian should play a proactive role in collaborating with teaching faculty in designing assignments and even syllabi to facilitate the best learning possible for students. Finally, whether library users are on campus or at a distance, they should receive the same consideration and service. Distance learners should be provided as many of the same services and resources as possible as on-campus library users. It is the challenge and the reward of academic libraries to extend their mission beyond the library walls.

Among the key responsibilities of academic librarians is one that is often neglected because of time and staffing constraints: assessment. When libraries and librarians neglect to assess what they're doing, they can easily assume that their priorities meet users' priorities and needs, but actually be off base in their assumptions. Assessment, including self-assessment and self-reflection upon oneself as a practitioner, is essential to sustained success. Unless libraries engage with constituencies, both informally and formally, to determine whether they're meeting user needs, they cannot grow and evolve adequately with the changing nature of the learning environment, nor can they meet the needs of the learner sufficiently.[4]

More than ever before, the land grant university reference librarian has the opportunity to actively engage and help facilitate both the immediate and the lifelong learning of library constituencies, primarily students. While technological advances allow easier and quicker access to information, they also serve to heighten the important role of librarians as educators. The issue of finding enough information has turned into an issue of sifting through too much information in order to find the most relevant while learning what resources are appropriate for which kinds of information, as well as how to access the needed information. The 21st-century reference librarian is the intermediary between the library user and the information resources. However, reference librarians cannot sit back and wait for information seekers to come to them. Reference librarians everywhere, and especially those at land grant universities, the people's universities, must be proactive in helping users to fulfill their information needs. Enthusiastic and skillful research assistance will gratify library users, keep them coming back, and ensure their support of the institution and the library profession well into the future.

NOTES

1. George R. McDowell, *Land Grant Universities and Extension into the 21st Century: Renegotiating or Abandoning a Social Contract* (Ames, IA: Iowa State University Press, 2001).

2. Hannelore B. Rader, "A New Academic Library Model: Partnerships for Learning and Teaching," *C & RL News* 62 (2001): 393–96.

3. Helen H. Spaulding, Deborah Abston, and Mark Cain, "Only Change Is Constant: Three Librarians Consider What Their Jobs Will Be Like in Five Years," *C & RL News* 59 (1998): 601–03.

4. Kellogg Commission on the Future of State and Land-Grant Universities. 2001. *Returning to Our Roots: Executive Summaries of the Reports of the Kellogg Commission on the Future of State and Land-Grant Universities* [online]. New York: National Association of State Universities and Land-Grant Colleges. Office of Public Affairs [cited 28 July 2001]. Available online at http://www.nasulgc.org.

2

John Henry's Dilemma

Philip Swan

The successful librarian of the 21st century must argue for the relevancy of the profession in a way none of his or her predecessors were required to. In a dilemma worthy of John Henry, librarians find themselves competing with lightning-fast computers and other electronic gadgetry for the hearts and minds of the information-gathering public. At the turn of the century we find ourselves competing chiefly with the Internet. The days when librarians were among the few individuals in the community to understand what the Internet could do are rapidly diminishing, and a new generation has come of age with the Internet as much a part of their lives as television. How, then, do we maintain our relevance in this new information-driven age?

The answer lies in the definition of information. For the average patrons, information is increasingly encompassed by what they can dredge up from the Internet in fifteen minutes. In this sense, information taken from the Internet is like fast food: it is quick, easy to appreciate, and convenient. We, as librarians, need to offer more nutritious fare. A hamburger under a heating lamp will fill you up as readily as filet mignon, but you go to a nice restaurant because the food will be better made, the variety will be greater, the atmosphere will be richer, and the staff will treat you as an individual, with care and warmth. We are the maitre d's of the best information bistros in town; the trick is to get the public to value the benefits of savoring a good meal, expertly prepared.

Like a master chef pondering a variety of ingredients, a librarian must be able to draw on a broad knowledge of both print and electronic resources in order to hit upon a combination that creates something successful out of their synthesis. Unfortunately, with electronic resources burgeoning to a dizzying extent, librarians are often tempted to allow online databases to supplant the print resources they were intended to supplement. We are, in a way, allowing technology to do the thinking for us, and, in the process, we are ultimately doing a disservice both to our patrons and the profession. We must be mindful of print sources and other traditional forms of information that are still as relevant as they ever were, and somehow find a way to incorporate these resources with the ever-changing nature of electronic information gathering. The key is to remember that this process is pliant—begging to be explored in a variety of ways that take both the librarian and the patron on a mutually satisfying voyage of intellectual discovery.

If we are to avoid becoming information automatons, we must be intellectually engaged. We are infinitely superior to computers because we can combine tremendous creativity with insatiable curiosity. The best librarians I have worked with all had one thing in common: an innate need to resolve the questions posed to them by patrons and the willingness to go about doing so by any means at their disposal. It is this need to get at answers that makes librarianship a vocation and not simply a job.

It is telling to see a librarian become aggravated by patrons because they ask difficult questions and are persistent in finding an answer. The patron's refusal to accept a facile answer annoys those librarians who undoubtedly harbor guilty feelings for not being as passionate about information retrieval as they know they should be. Pointing, for these librarians, with either mouse or finger, is the extent of their perception of their responsibility to the patron, and the desk they sit behind is rarely empty for even a moment. How can we expect our patrons to value our profession when we are doing something they can do themselves on their home PCs?

This gets us to the other essential issue for librarians in the 21st century; the relationship between librarian and patron. If we possess the creativity and curiosity a machine lacks, we sometimes, ironically, lack its social graces. Computer terminals are never impatient, irritable or judgmental. A great opportunity is being lost when librarians fail to build even rudimentary relationships with the people they serve. An unspoken truism among librarians is that many are not personable—seemingly going out of their way to avoid human contact of any kind if at all possible. Too often, this attitude takes the shape of outright misanthropy or an easy cynicism that gives short shrift to patrons who come to us for personal assistance. It is incumbent upon us as librarians to ensure that the library remains an attractive alternative to a night in front of a television or a computer screen. In short, if you do not enjoy interacting with people, you will never be happy as a librarian. Keep in mind, there is always room for one more behind those fast-food counters.

3

Out of the Box

Marie Jones

As we hire librarians in the coming century, we must first remember that libraries are no longer contained within the physical walls of our library buildings. Because of the needs of distance education, academic libraries may have been the first to break down those walls, but the demand for at-home access to library materials is being felt in all types of libraries. If people can sit at their home computer and access the Internet, why can't they also sit at home and access all of the wonderful worlds of information and entertainment available in their local library? Can library materials be ordered online and delivered to their doorstep the way everything from groceries to automobiles now can be?

With this premise in mind, what does it take to be an excellent librarian in a library-without-walls? Flexibility. Innovation. Awareness of current innovations, trends, and public interests. Alongside the same skills and interests librarians have always had: organization, critical thinking, a strong service orientation, and a true devotion to the people we serve.

Where, you ask, is technological ability in that list? In a virtual library, won't library professionals need lots of computer skills? Of course. Technological ability is in the same place as knowing the LC or Dewey classification system. It's a given absolute expectation of every school of library and information science graduate. A really excellent librarian will not only have the basic computer skills, but will know how to update those skills as needs rapidly change during the course of a career. A really excellent librarian will not only know how to use technology, but will have a vision of how technology is likely to change over the coming years and what influence those changes will have on current investments and decisions.

The best librarians will know where the balance should fall between solid, old-fashioned librarianship in which libraries are organized storehouses for information dissemination and whiz-bang electronic librarianship where vendors own everything and we just help people get to it. For every library, that balance will be different. It's important that librarians have the critical thinking skills necessary to know where the balance point is for their libraries. One of the essential missions of libraries is to reduce the information gap between the "haves" and the "have-nots." This mission and its implementation in a specific library helps define that library's balance points, as do whatever other goals are part of the library's mission statement.

That strong service orientation I mentioned earlier becomes vital as we take libraries out of the building box. If people don't walk in the door to a library as often as they used to, they don't see that friendly librarian waiting and willing to answer their questions. They don't have a librarian sneak up on them and ask if they need help when they start to look lost. They don't have the physical comfort of the smell of old books and cozy chairs to make the library seem like a homey place to curl up and read. Librarians, then, must be more proactive in providing service, training, and doing PR. New and innovative approaches must be implemented in order to maintain traditional standards of service excellence.

Being proactive may be the ultimate key to 21st century librarianship. Those outside the profession may see librarians as being a bunch of sleepy conservatives surrounded by books. The last few decades have shown the profession to actually be one that is on the cutting edge, looking ahead to the future and applying to it the vast knowledge gained over the years. As information technology continues to bound ahead during this century, librarians must keep up with the trends, both in technology and in the rapidly changing profession of librarianship.

So what librarians should we hire in the 21st century? Skilled, intelligent, friendly experienced people. When we hire people new to the profession, we need to mentor them to help them become wisely experienced. We must hire librarians that show balance and forethought, optimism and caring, innovation and a solid sense of each library's mission. We must hire people who can learn. People we'd like to work with. Great librarians.

4

The Curious Librarian

Kenneth A. Smith

I am a reference librarian in an academic library. Though this perspective informs what I have to say, I believe my advice is relevant to other librarians working in other types of libraries. In addition to being a reference librarian, I am also the "Electronic Resources Librarian" at my institution. I mention this because I don't want to be taken as anti-technology. I recognize the value of technology. I have a facility for it, and most of the time, I even enjoy it. Nonetheless, I believe technology and technological skills tend to be overemphasized. What characteristics would I look for in a new library hire?

In a word, I suggest hiring someone *curious*. First of all, curiosity is itself a marker of intelligence. Secondly and more importantly, the habits of curiosity, exploration and learning, make for a knowledgeable person with perennially up-to-date skills. Don't be overly impressed if a candidate knows the latest software or has experience in some trendy new area of service! These are transient advantages. In the long run the person of lively and omnivorous interests will be the more successful librarian.

In general, there is too much focus on technique and technology in the field of librarianship. What tends to get overlooked is the importance of creativity and active intelligence. The best librarians make surprising connections between one topic and another. They can rephrase questions in ways that invite new perspectives. It's not all a matter of knowing *how* or where to search for something. Often enough, it's a matter of knowing *what else* to explore. ("You should also try. . . .") In this regard, the role of intellect, knowledge and creativity are tremendously important. If librarianship could be boiled down to technique, then I assure you, technology will replace librarians.

So how, within the context of a typical job interview, can you determine a candidate's curiosity level? At the end of this essay I've outlined a few ideas: some questions and behaviors to look for. However, there's no question here of *measuring* curiosity. The questions are meant as investigatory aids, to help you "feel out" the candidates. In the end you must rely on your judgment. But doesn't this involve a strong possibility of bias? Isn't it possible that men, for example, will tend to be rated higher for curiosity?

Clearly, there is a potential for bias. One reason technological skills get emphasized is precisely the desire for objective hiring criteria. And yet hiring decisions are so complex that "judgment" is almost always called on. I've seen a candidate rejected because he or she didn't seem very interested in the job. Exactly how disinterest was communicated is not clear. It was possible to identify an instance or two to support this perception, and yet these instances were in themselves ambiguous. Nonetheless, everyone on the search committee shared the perception that the candidate was not especially interested in the position.

Our intuitive sense of people, though fallible and subject to bias, is nonetheless highly sophisticated. Instead of trying to eliminate such judgments (yet secretly relying on them), it is better to bring them to the fore. We can then subject these perceptions to corrective criticism. To control for bias I suggest two things. First, maintain a high level of critical awareness. Take note if you find yourself liking or disliking the candidate. Take note if he or she is confident or extroverted. It's possible to confuse these traits with curiosity. On the other hand you should take note if the candidate is highly nervous or shy. Such traits can obscure curiosity. Secondly, I would emphasize the need for a diverse search committee. Conflicting perceptions may indicate the operation of bias, and they need to be hashed out. A diverse committee membership ensures that many biases will be checked.

I don't want to give the impression that curiosity is the only important quality a candidate need possess. After all, you want to hire someone to work, not to learn about work. If undisciplined, high levels of curiosity will only produce irresponsible eccentrics. However, in a competitive job market, curiosity might well be the factor that separates the ordinary from the extraordinary candidate.

The role of knowledge merits a comment. (In large part curiosity is important because curious people are constantly adding to their knowledge base.) The best background a librarian can have is a good general education, and you should look for this in your candidates. By a general education I mean a broad rather than a specialized education. Ideally the candidate will have some familiarity with all disciplinary types: the sciences, the social sciences and the humanities. As the skills and competencies necessary for effective librarianship increase, I hope the profession will resist the temptation to establish undergraduate programs. Future librarians are better served by a broad education, and the undergraduate program is their best opportunity to get one.

Here are some general things to look for in doing an interview:

Questions

- Does the candidate ask a lot of questions?
- Does the candidate ask spontaneous questions, unrelated to the position, institution, or immediate community (e.g., an architectural feature)?

Probe Interests

- What is their interest in the position? Does their interest include the opportunity for further learning?
- What was their favorite [non-] library science course? Why?
- What is their favorite reference work? Why?
- Ask them, "Can you tell us something you recently learned, or learned about, while on the job?"
- Ask about interests and hobbies.

Behavior

- Watch carefully during the library tour. Try meeting them (or leaving them) by the reference collection, new books shelf, etc. Do they scan titles, poke around, etc.?
- During the period of the interview do they take time to explore, by themselves, the library, its resources (such as workstations), the campus, the community?

In closing, let me reiterate: look for signs of curiosity in your candidates. Curiosity reflects intelligence, which is important per se. But it also reflects something of even more importance: the values and habits of learning. Are the candidates those who will seek out new knowledge? Will they browse and "try out" new reference books? Will they "play" with new databases and applications? Will they take the time to do these things even when they are busy? They will, if they are curious.

5

Of Babies and Bathwater—Hiring Library Staff for the 21st Century

Danelle Hall

In the article, "Wanted: Library Leaders for a Discontinuous Future" in the January 2001 issue of *Library Issues,* author Terry Metz proposes that the entire profession of librarianship is in a dramatic state of change, that change will be with us into the foreseeable future, and that librarians, especially their leaders, will have to learn to function in a new environment. A slightly more helpful article, "Cyber or Siberia? Library skills in transition," by Gordon Dunsire in the January/February 2001 issue of *IMPACT,*[1] discusses actual changes in the skills needed now to run a library. Mr. Dunsire sees a diminishing need for clerical skills and paraprofessional skills in a library. He sees the role of the library employee evolving from being a caretaker of physical items such as books and videos into being a specialist in training and educating users in the use of the new information resources. Carla Stoffle comments that "Today's challenges create a dynamic environment unlike any that academic librarians have ever experienced. For this reason it has become necessary for librarians to reinvent ourselves so we can best serve our communities."[2]

If I am to believe these authors, not only do I have constant turmoil and change to look forward to as a library leader, but also the very heart of my profession will be redesigned to meet the challenges of the new millennium. While the role of teacher is not foreign to librarians, the idea of discarding or "reinventing" the role of information provider disturbs me.

From ancient times, libraries have faced change. We changed from clay tablets to papyrus scrolls to sheets of paper to bound books. We moved from the stylus to the quill pen to the printing press. We now have moved to the electronic document. Through all of these changes, however, the core of the profession remained the same with its basic responsibility to preserve knowledge and deliver it to the person who needs it. If the core of our profession changes, this will have a significant impact on the skills of those we recruit and hire.

In looking at all of the new information sources and thinking about the staff needed to manage them, I remind myself that a library is created slowly over time and from many sources. We have new information sources. We also have old sources that are still valuable. Perhaps we don't have to assume an "all or nothing at all" stance. Perhaps the professional stance over the next few years should be one of reassessing rather than reinventing ourselves.

Undoubtedly, the information landscape is changing. Undoubtedly, there are many resources that a person can turn to at home twenty-four hours a day, seven days a week, and training would help the person find and use these sources more effectively. Undoubtedly there are uninformed people who assume that the Internet replaces libraries. There are also occasions when a patron needs the skilled help of a librarian whether using traditional print sources or searching the Internet.

So as the library director at a small, private, Midwestern university, what should I be seeking in a new hire? Given my philosophical leanings, I will be looking for someone skilled with the new technologies but with a deep appreciation of the ancient calling of librarianship. To move from the philosophical realm to the practical, I will have some basic expectations of any library candidate regardless of the direction our profession finally takes:

1. He or she will have worked with computers and be comfortable with computers.
2. He or she will be able to create word-processing documents.
3. He or she will be able to use e-mail comfortably, attach documents and forward messages and reply to messages.

These skills are the equivalent of being able to type and having a pleasant telephone manner in earlier days. If I find an applicant with additional skills with programs such as Access or Excel I will be delighted.

The professional librarian/library faculty member should be current in knowledge of the state of the profession. He or she should be a problem solver, and be able to see the whole picture and how the pieces fit together. Intellectual curiosity and the ability to find creative solutions are essential to a librarian.

Even in this world in transition, the personal qualities I look for in an employee have not changed since my grandfather's time:

1. Honesty
2. Integrity
3. Accuracy
4. The ability to empathize and sympathize with others as they cope with the stresses of the workplace.
5. I want an employee who listens and actually hears what is said.
6. I want an employee who "helps."

To staff the libraries of the 21st century, to manage and control our information-rich environment we need staff with sophisticated technical skills. We need staff with the tried and true personal values from a simpler time. Finally, we need staff with the willingness to help. They need to be able to help our patrons learn to find their way through the glut of information available to them. They need to be able to help the profession reassess or reinvent itself.

Change has come, and is still coming. Our future, we have already agreed, will most likely be "discontinuous." It is important to remain flexible and open to possibilities both as we confront the needs of our profession and as we hire our staff for the future. While it is tempting to jump on the hype bandwagon and proclaim the arrival of the new information age complete with refurbished profession, moderation is never out of style.

For now, the bathwater can go, but not the baby.

NOTES

1. http://www.careerdevelopmentgroup.org.uk/impact/.
2. *C&RL NEWS* 61 (2000): 894.

6

Going to Town

Interviewing in the Large Urban Public Library

Alison Hopkins

I enjoy interviewing librarian candidates. Since I began interviewing regularly, about two years ago, I have learned a lot about myself and about the interviewing process. Every interview is an opportunity to be reenergized by the enthusiasm of someone just starting out in the library field and the potential to meet a future library director. Last year, I interviewed approximately 100 candidates interested in positions in a large urban public library. The questions I ask during an interview have evolved over time, and reflect changing expectations from just two years ago. Interestingly enough, I find that the minimum qualifications have changed the most, while the qualities that allow me to differentiate between candidates have remained much the same.

When I start an interview, my initial questions are fairly general, and then quickly focus on determining the candidate's knowledge of what I consider basic librarian skills. These basic skills include how to do a reference interview, familiarity with some basic reference resources, and the ability to evaluate books from a collection development standpoint. I expect familiarity with professional terms and current debates within the world of librarianship.

In the last few years, I have noticed more of an emphasis on technology, especially the Internet, from librarian candidates. I now expect that any entry-level applicant should know how to search the Web, has looked at my library's website, and can evaluate different websites. In the future, I expect that candidates will continue to be conversant in the latest format, whether that is e-books or something else altogether.

Yet, I have still hired entry-level candidates who were not Web experts. If candidates can use some sort of software, are willing to learn, and have other, rarer skills, I have hired them and they have been successful on the job.

It takes much more than the basic librarian skills to be a librarian in a public library. I believe that the public library fills a special place in a community. The library is a vibrant part of the community, a meeting place, a place to go for information, for entertainment, and for cultural activity. It reflects the changing and diverse interests of the community as well as its history. To be a successful librarian in a public library means being interested in serving, changing, and learning. The best public librarians become an important part of the community, learning what people want and providing it in changing times. Finding people who fit this ideal can be difficult.

As an interviewer, I have had to break down the qualities that I believe make a good public librarian. These include a strong interest in providing good customer service, good communication skills, and familiarity with best-selling fiction and nonfiction.

My ideal candidate has some customer service experience, preferably in a very busy and occasionally challenging environment. This candidate has dealt with difficult situations and can describe them to me. In his or her description, I look for consideration for both the customer and the company, and patience when handling the situation. A candidate with this kind of customer service experience who expresses interest in helping others is perfect for the busy and demanding reference desks of a public library.

Candidates without this kind of experience must express interest in helping others. I look for candidates who understand the mission of a public library and who express it passionately. Communication skills are also very important. Language skills are especially useful, as is knowledge of a particular community or culture.

My ideal candidate is familiar with a variety of literature, especially best-selling and genre fiction. Preferably the candidate enjoys reading and can discuss some best-selling fiction or nonfiction with enthusiasm. Much of the business done at my library system involves the recommendation of reading material and the sharing of good books to read. The ideal readers' advisory librarian has knowledge of a variety of genres, knows the best-selling books, including nonfiction, and can recommend something similar in a friendly, sharing manner. Readers' advisory builds a connection between the librarian and the reader, as someone who can share and recommend books becomes a friend.

In the 21st century and beyond, I expect that the skills needed to find information will change. The format of information storage has the potential to change in the future, and librarians will need to be able to use these different formats. But the most important skills for a public librarian have not changed, and I expect that in the future those skills will become even more important. As public libraries continue to offer recreational, educational and informational resources to the communities they serve, good customer service and communication skills as well as book knowledge will continue to be invaluable. It is with these skills that librarians build connections to their communities and are able to meet their ever-changing needs.

7

"Stand Back," Said the Elephant, "I'm Going to Sneeze!"

Janice Krueger

Children's literature often provides the adult reader with enjoyment, relaxation, and a humorous way of regarding one's situation in life. The varied characters, drawings, fantasies, and events have a way of traversing time and offering a refreshing alternative to stressful and demanding adult responsibilities. One group of responsibilities, in particular, involves career and employment obligations. Current and projected future demands of librarianship can be viewed in this light.

When reflecting on the myriad responsibilities for an academic librarian, *The 500 Hats of Bartholomew Cubbins* by Dr. Seuss comes to mind. When Bartholomew removed one hat, another grew in its place. Likewise, librarians not only wear many hats, but "grow" new ones as the need arises or, more appropriately, as technology dictates. Not only are the traditional roles of academic librarianship maintained, but also new titles, or positions, are taken on and developed. The usual responsibilities for collection development, management of the public service areas, teaching commitments, and public service hours at the reference desk are interwoven with new demands. Positions created a few years ago for acquiring and maintaining electronic databases metamorphose to include Web page development, enhancement, administration, and electronic reserves. An instruction position evolves into an outreach and marketing position and all find themselves scratching their heads for new ways to publicize and "sell" library services, much the same as the peddler and the monkeys in Esphyr Slobodkina's *Caps for Sale*. Academic librarians are overwhelming required to be teachers, computer technicians, salespersons, politicians, researchers, and investigators, to say the least.

All don their teaching hats when delivering instruction sessions requested by professors, implement programs to incorporate information competencies in curriculums, suggest materials for courses and assignments, and by personally interacting with students as their research needs dictate throughout a course. Reference librarians wear their technician hat, when they are required to be, in varying degrees, Web page developers for liaison areas, solvers of printing, networking, and computer problems, and well versed in computer applications involving e-mail, word processing, spreadsheets, databases, and statistical packages.

Academic librarians put on their sales chapeau when they struggle to find new ways to attract students to library resources and advertise all those expensive databases that expand the gold mine of information students think they can locate on the Internet. The politician hat is worn when dealing with conflicting needs between students, between students and faculty, between students, faculty, alumni and policy, and when negotiating for a place in a department's outcomes, goals, or, at least, a spotlight on the syllabus. Researcher attire is appropriate when designing new and creative surveys and studies that both evaluate resources and services for effectiveness and lure student participation in the fashion of Tom Sawyer.

When all is said and done, however, the most prominent hat by far is that of investigator, or private eye, otherwise known as Sherlock Holmes, or Encyclopedia Brown's thinking cap. This is worn daily as databases are analyzed, classes are planned, new information resources are sought and examined, and when tackling reference questions that do not fit into a predefined book or website. Sleuthing through the stacks, virtual or otherwise, is a high priority. Today's successful librarian and tomorrow's future librarian must remain open to investigating new end products, new search engines, new websites, new ways of handling and storing information, new ways of communicating, and new ways of delivering reference services.

Librarians have come a long way in redefining their profession and raising it to a prominent position in the information business. That position will reach its pinnacle as long as the field develops with technology, the Internet, or whatever new conduit is created to find, organize, and deliver information. It is more enjoyable if it is perceived less as a challenge and more like a dance with technology, much the same as the grandfather in Karen Ackerman's *Song and Dance Man*. Just as librarians feel they finally have arrived or "got it," one can hear the loud cry emanating from *"Stand Back," Said the Elephant, "I'm Going to Sneeze!"*

REFERENCES

Ackerman, Karen. *Song and Dance Man* (New York: Alfred A. Knopf, 1988).

Seuss, Dr. [Theodor Seuss Geisel]. *The 500 Hats of Bartholomew Cubbins* (New York: Random House, 1965).

Slobodkina, Esphyr. *Caps for Sale* (New York: HarperCollins, 1968).

Thomas, Patricia. *"Stand Back," Said the Elephant, "I'm Going to Sneeze!"* (New York: Lothrop, Lee & Shepard Books, 1990).

8

The Cooperative Librarian

Jennifer Inglis

Turning to someone else for help is a natural human response. It is often the basis for someone seeking assistance at the library or from a librarian. It is the footing for giving this assistance as well. Although the origin and definition of the word "librarian," keeper of a library, in no way indicate sharing or altruism, the essence of library service in the 21st century is a spirit of collective and cooperative action.

Consider this. No one person can know everything or have enough items or access to enough data to meet all information needs. This shortage of intellectual, physical or electronic resources forces people to turn to others for assistance. Many times those "others" are librarians. In the same way, individual librarians and libraries habitually turn to each other to meet their and their users' needs.

Like a pebble in a pond, the reference interview frequently sets in motion a series of human and organizational interactions. The librarian uses his or her training and various tools to try to meet the user's need. If the librarian is unsuccessful, time and again he or she enlists the aid of a colleague. That person may, after reaching the end of his or her expertise, refer the patron to someone or some other department elsewhere within the institution.

Some needs cannot be met by the library at all. Regularly there comes a point during a reference interview when a patron must be referred to an organization that provides services beyond the scope of the library. At that point, the librarian's work interfaces with other agencies, thereby extending the cooperative spirit of information provision beyond the walls of the library to the community.

In a small library, librarians are particularly dependent upon each other's shared knowledge of general and specific subjects, drawing on each other's combined education and life experience to assist patrons. The simple act of providing directions or being aware of local activities are prime examples of this.

In larger library systems, collaborative effort translates into cross-department or multi-branch assistance. When a question moves beyond the scope of a particular subject or service department, the user can often be referred elsewhere within the system.

Institutionally, we work together to meet the needs of our users through various forms of resource sharing. Interlibrary loan agreements are traditional examples of this, whereas collective buying contracts are a more recent development reflecting our need and ability to work together.

The essence of this idea is that we, as individuals and organizations, turn to others to meet our needs so that we, in turn, may meet the needs of our users. We act as one another's mentors, assistants and teammates, trading off patrons and working with the satisfaction of the user in mind. I, for one, could not succeed in this arena without this supportive net.

From where I sit writing this piece, I look out on a bank of computers and stacks of reference material that are impressive to the untrained eye. In reality, the collection is quite limited. How can I possibly assist our patrons given this situation?

It is how we, as librarians, use our resources and tools, which include one another, that make circumstances such as this work. I cannot possibly know all that is in even our tiny reference collection, but I have the skills to know how to use it, the tools to search it, and the co-workers who know parts of it that I do not.

When I transferred from a neighborhood branch to a subject department of an urban public library system, I had to learn the basic research tools for law, genealogy, cartography, and fund-raising. When the scope of a question went beyond my expertise, I could usually turn to a colleague who either specialized in that subject area or had been in the department long enough to know which tool to use. He or she suggested a resource or took over the question entirely, depending upon the situation.

In my current small college library setting, the staff members wear many hats. Our life experiences go a long way toward helping us perform our jobs and support one another as co-workers. The current director's many years of study and training in music allow him to easily handle questions from music faculty that stump me. My years of work in newspapers and public libraries allow me to recommend and provide services that my colleagues had not previously considered. Our former director had not only expertise in philosophy and religion but a personal essence that brought a calming influence to the jumpy shores of our little world.

Support staff members are integral to this joint endeavor that we call library service. As an alumnus of our college, one of our support staff members is a valuable source of information on the college's administrative, academic and social history. The other staff member puts to use her personal experience with bookkeeping systems to effectively manage our acquisitions process. Our small, varied staff illustrates how the whole is greater than the sum of its parts.

The librarian who cannot or will not admit his or her limits and turn to his or her colleagues is the stumbling block upon which library service will fail. It is our profession's willingness to serve and our ability to work together in a cooperative spirit—a sublimation of ego, if you will—that allows us to do what we do.

Given the vast array of items and data available, how can we connect the user with that which he or she needs? By asking for help. Our patrons do it. We do it, too. From query files developed over the years by our predecessors, to support staff who know how to obtain the most recent copy of an item, library service is an intrinsically interdependent human function. Without our ability to work together, libraries and librarians would be isolated and ineffectual purveyors of data. With it, we represent the best of the cooperative human spirit.

9

Mere Mortals Need Not Apply

Jane Birks and Liz Oesleby

As the 21st century begins, academic librarians face renewed challenges in their role of providing traditional information services in a rapidly changing world. We are all aware of the impact which technological advances have made on our field. The challenges to academic librarians, however, go further than managing the changes in technology. Just as great a challenge is created by the shift in focus of our role as information providers. The academic librarian has, in the past, been an intermediary between the information and the seeker of that information while teaching has been the domain of the faculty. Today, however, those roles are changing. Today the user interfaces directly with the information. The librarian assumes the role of instructor. As part of this new role, the academic librarian must now identify specific competencies that the user needs to access information and must develop strategies to help users acquire these competencies.

The mandate for academic librarians today is instruction; they are no longer simply handing out information. The instructional role is now as great or even greater than the traditional reference role. A new type of librarian has entered the playing field. The "information literacy librarian" has assumed an important role on the public services team.

Why does an academic institution consider information literacy so vital to its mission? Students today are often overwhelmed by information and by their ability to handle it. As Henri and Bonanno observe: "Throughout history the trend has been towards faster and faster production of information, faster transmission of information, more compact storage of information—but our capacity to read and understand information remains constant."[1]

Today's university graduates must have suitable strategies for handling such a flood of information. The obvious provider of these strategies is the library's information literacy librarian. What implications does this have for a director hiring librarians for the cutting-edge academic library?

A modern library director needs a librarian who can assume responsibility for development and implementation of an information literacy program. According to the American Library Association (ALA), information literacy is the ability to identify information needs, access and evaluate appropriate information and communicate effectively to meet those needs. It is more than traditional bibliographic instruction. It is more than knowledge of Library of Congress Classification, more than finding a book on the shelves, or using an index or specialized reference work. Information literacy requires a sequential development of the research process itself. Information literacy incorporates, but is not limited to, concepts previously included in bibliographic instruction. The information literacy librarian must be capable of developing a curriculum as well as integrating it into the larger academic structure.[2]

The director needs a librarian with qualifications in learning theory and practice as well as experience in classroom teaching. This librarian will understand the implications of learning styles, individual differences, attention spans, adult learning techniques, teaching English to speakers of other languages (TESOL) theory and techniques, and outcomes-based education. This ideal librarian actually enjoys teaching . . . and is good at it!

The director should be considering only candidates who are well organized, able to undertake long-range planning, develop curriculum and set both short- and long-term objectives. The successful candidate can envision a program, develop the steps to put it in place, implement the program, and finally evaluate the program's success.

The ideal librarian's background in all aspects of public service ensures an understanding of the role information literacy plays in fulfilling the library's mission. This librarian has kept up with the surge of rapidly changing technology. This librarian is comfortable with the variety of applications used in an academic library such as the concept of digitized collections, the use of online databases and evaluation of Web-based resources.

Development of information literacy is a continuing process, so many of the skills need to be introduced at a simple level and reinforced at increasingly sophisticated levels to develop depth as the student progresses through his or her studies. The director needs a librarian who is able to integrate these library-based skills into the academic curriculum—both across the content of the curriculum and at various levels of instruction.

The information literacy librarian needs to be a contributing member of the library team, able to work with library staff and administration to ensure that the information literacy program is an integral part of the overall library mission. This librarian must also act as a library's liaison to academic units to raise awareness about information literacy, to develop consultation and instruction which will ensure integration of information literacy into the curriculum, and to support resource selection and collection development to support curriculum development.

The director might place the following notice:

CUTTING-EDGE UNIVERSITY

Library

Job Description

Seeking "SuperLib" for the position of information literacy librarian at a dynamic academic institution committed to providing quality service to students, faculty and staff.

Qualifications:

Must have an MLS from an accredited institution with a minimum of three years' postgraduate experience and a second master's degree in the field of education with a minimum of three years' successful classroom teaching. Competency with all aspects of information technology essential.

Able to lead, coordinate and participate in the library's overall instruction program. Should have demonstrated ability to develop curriculum. Enjoys teaching (no dry lecturers need apply). A team player able to work successfully with library staff and interface with the university's academic units.

Personal strengths: organized self-starter stronger than a determined dean, faster than changing technology, able to leap tall bookstacks in a single bound.

Library's state-of-the-art security system provides Kryptonite protection.

Mere mortals need not apply.

NOTES

1. James Henri, and Karen Bonanno, *The Information Literate School Community: Best Practice* (Wagga Wagga, Australia: Center for Information Studies, 1999).

2. American Library Association, "Presidential Committee on Information Literacy," October 1, 1989; Association of College & Research Libraries, November 3, 2001. Available online at http://www.ala.org/acrl/nili/ilit1st.html.

10

We're Looking for a Few Good Catalogers

Bridgette Scott

I joined the dark side in library school—I became a cataloger. When I announced my intentions to devote my career to MARC, LCSH, and LCRIs, my friends and mentors bestowed upon me looks of mixed incredulity and dismay. After all, catalogers were the outcasts of library school—they were the rule-loving loners who would be dispatched upon graduation to dusty basement offices and card catalogs. But I would not be dissuaded. I knew that cataloging in the 21st century encompassed so much more than the stereotypical image of typewriters, 3 × 5 cards, and books of convoluted rules. Technology changed cataloging into something much greater. Now catalogers work on a global stage, organizing vast stores of information, providing access to intangible digital creations, and creating complex structural databases. Recognizing this was a stroke of luck for me, enabling me to become part of one of the most innovative and dynamic areas of librarianship.

How do you know if you are cut out to be a cataloger? Job advertisements ask for knowledge of automation systems, MARC encoding, classification schemes, and subject headings. But it is important to remember that these are all skills that can be acquired. For entry-level catalogers, what is more crucial is that the cataloger possess a certain set of personal characteristics.

The successful cataloger will be a problem solver. Problems arise in all sorts and shapes in technical services, ranging from tracking down and fixing past cataloging mistakes to deciding what to do with a new collection of archival photographs. Assigning subject headings and call numbers requires the ability to assess the content of an item and determine not only how it relates to other items, but also what makes it unique. Then there is the fact that no matter how comprehensive the rules for cataloging may seem, there are always items that fall through the cracks. If you would embrace the challenge of providing access to a book with no title page, or a magazine that changes its name every month, then cataloging is for you.

A good cataloger will be flexible. The cataloging profession is packed with rules, rule interpretations, rule modifications, and proposals for new rules. But as crucial as these instructions are, there are times when it is just as important to know how to bend the rules without breaking them. Finding a way to slide in information that the rules do not allow for can mean the difference between relegating an item to obscurity, or making it accessible for a doctoral student's dissertation. In addition, catalogers need flexibility to catalog in an increasingly digital environment. Catalogers now provide access to databases, websites, electronic books, CD-ROMs, DVDs, and a host of other digital formats. They do so using online documentation and automated catalogs, with e-mail and cataloging software to assist them. If you long to provide stability in a world of shifting technology, changing rules, and developing formats, then cataloging is for you.

Catalogers must have a strong service orientation. The most important rule to remember in cataloging is that the users' needs come first. Being able to bend your mind to think of all the ways your particular users might look for an item is essential for good cataloging. This means communicating with reference librarians to find out how their patrons are searching, discussing cataloging techniques with librarians in other libraries, and even talking with the patrons themselves. After all, the primary purpose of a library catalog is to point library users to relevant materials. If you are tantalized by the idea of making it easier for a chef to find the appropriate cookbook or a lawyer to find the pertinent statute, then cataloging is for you.

Contrary to popular belief, then, cataloging does not require an obsession with minutiae or a tendency toward rigidity. What they don't teach you in library school is that being a good cataloger demands more than mere adherence to AACR2, knowledge of subject headings, and familiarity with automation systems. The most important aspects of cataloging are the ones that cannot be taught—the logical mind that loves to tackle problems, the flexible personality that can invent creative solutions out of a sea of technology, and the solid dedication to helping people find what they want in the library. In the end, this means that cataloging is not for everyone—is it for you?

11

Hiring Academic Reference Librarians in the 21st Century

Mary M. Nofsinger

It is a challenge to thrive in the current academic reference environment due to limited budgets, demands for accountability, constantly changing technologies, and pressures to provide information faster, better, anywhere, and anytime. As a result, these essential characteristics have become vital for newly hired librarians.

OPTIMISM AND ENTHUSIASM

Librarians who expect positive outcomes, even in the face of difficulty, and who are highly motivated to provide personal, individually tailored reference assistance are assets in an academic environment. Those who are excited about working with both traditional and digital information resources will have to resolve numerous challenges since change is accelerating. Proactive reference librarians with an enthusiastic service orientation will find it easier to approach customers to deliver high-quality reference and instructional services regardless of complexity, format, or location.

FLEXIBILITY AND CREATIVITY

Reference librarians who embrace change and adapt to new realities as they appear will thrive in the 21st century. As the racial, ethnic, and cultural makeup of the U.S. population shifts, librarians will be working with new constituencies. Those who are flexible will develop an understanding and appreciation for cultural differences in order to successfully meet the needs of diverse customers and co-workers. Academic reference librarians will also need to become more sensitive to issues related to customers' learning styles. Furthermore, librarians must be creative as their roles shift, as digital collections expand, and as physical access and delivery methods expand the flow of information to independent learners on and off campus. Digital reference interviews and collaborative 24/7 reference services will demand flexible and creative responses as well as strong critical thinking and problem-solving skills.

COURAGE

To be successful in the 21st century, reference librarians will need to take risks, be assertive, and experiment with new approaches—embracing approaches from outside the library world. Newly hired reference librarians must seriously challenge traditional librarianship values and priorities while weighing new assumptions. Many academic librarians are experimenting with pilot projects, focus groups, and other evaluative measures to get feedback from customers, to justify funding levels, and to avoid costly mistakes. Librarians also have to deal with sensitive political and social issues, including censorship, the digital divide, pornography, copyright, privacy and confidentiality concerns, intellectual freedom, and electronic archiving of resources.

ABILITY TO COMMUNICATE

Reference librarians who are articulate, persuasive, and use active listening will be most successful in querying customers to determine information needs, particularly if they are friendly and nonjudgmental, ask open-ended questions, and then follow up for customer satisfaction. Active listening allows a reference librarian to reflect on another person's message while soliciting feedback to better understand the speaker's frame of reference. A newly hired reference librarian can learn much from listening to customers and colleagues, avoiding mistakes and understanding the nature of problems before offering assistance. Articulate librarians also make effective presentations to teaching faculty and classes—teaching information retrieval and electronic manipulation skills essential in a digital world. Students who learn these skills will be competitive in the workplace and able to engage in lifelong learning. These teaching activities contribute to the research and instruction agendas of the campus.

ABILITY TO MARKET LIBRARY RESOURCES AND SERVICES

Academic librarians are ideally situated to publicize library resources and services to university customers. Proactive reference librarians will enhance library services by marketing their expertise and helping customers make effective use of these resources. Indeed, librarians MUST be involved in public relations and marketing if they are to survive in this competitive information age. Major corporations, Internet dot-coms, and other commercial competitors are already eagerly marketing their products in the higher education environment. If librarians publicize value-added services, such as electronic reserves, seamless access to electronic and print collections, assistance with integrating electronic resources into courses and course content, online tutorials, electronic notice of newly purchased materials, and quick guides to resources, they will enhance the relevance of library contributions to the university mission.

ABILITY TO BE A TEAM PLAYER

Newly hired reference librarians will need to develop collaborative partnerships with others to advance library goals, services, and programs. With colleagues, librarians need to share their knowledge and skills, and work as team members to analyze strategic goals, develop new initiatives, and set priorities. With faculty, librarians need to work cooperatively to provide assistance in the classroom and expertise with projects. With publishers, librarians need to negotiate consortial agreements to save money and to centralize services for customers' convenience. With computing professionals, librarians need to develop joint teaching programs and expand seamless access to electronic resources. New partnerships also extend the library's influence within the state and contribute to enhanced fund-raising efforts. Within the campus community, collaboration ensures that the mission of the library will remain viable in the 21st century.

CONFIDENCE AND SENSE OF HUMOR

Beginning librarians who understand their own strengths and weaknesses, and who have enough confidence to laugh at themselves and minor obstacles are usually successful in academic environments. As the nature of library work changes, self-confidence and a sense of humor help relieve stress and anxiety. A relaxed demeanor allows a librarian to focus more on customer needs, encourages productivity, and enhances the achievement of goals with less effort. These characteristics also encourage self-reliance, active learning, and professional activity. Self-motivated learners are highly valued in any workplace.

TECHNOLOGICAL COMPETENCE

Librarians with a strong technological background will be essential in creating 21st-century library collections and services. It is clear that full-text article databases, electronic books, chat-based interactive technologies, videoconferencing, voice-over-IP applications, and streaming media have already impacted the services and roles of reference librarians. Understanding these varied technologies, including imaging technologies, Web markup languages, metadata, user interface design, Internet searching, and multimedia will be essential. As this paradigm shift occurs reference librarians will be involved—developing seamless interfaces, help systems, delivering information to a variety of computing platforms, and coordinating this activity with computing and other personnel outside the library.

Forward-looking, dynamic academic libraries will be seeking these essential characteristics when hiring new reference librarians. Striving to meet the rapidly changing needs of society and higher education, librarians must continue to redefine their roles and emphasize new functions and services. Those librarians who can keep pace with these changes will be key players in the 21st-century academic library.

12

Librarians in the 21st Century

Barbara Lovato-Gassman

Librarians, prepare yourselves for the modern libraries/information centers of the 21st century. It has been energizing to learn how our profession is changing and evolving. As I read the requirements for admittance into library school, I thought to myself, "I need to be able to do what? HTML? FTP? Zip?" Library school isn't even the proper term anymore. Programs are calling themselves Schools of Information Resources and Library Science or Schools of Library and Information Management. But isn't that what libraries have always been about: collecting, managing and making available information and resources? Well, yes, but not quite the way it is done today.

In 1994, only seven short years ago, when I received my bachelor's degree, I had very little experience using computers. Even then, the extent of my computer aptitude was using the current word-processing program to prepare papers that I had researched "the old-fashioned way." When I entered library school three years later, I was not only expected to be computer literate, but I had to be able to navigate the Web proficiently, create Web pages, and communicate and learn in a completely virtual environment. Taking classes without ever seeing the instructor or my classmates in person was and continues to be a truly unique experience!

I must admit that it is more than a little disconcerting to be required to communicate, collaborate, learn, present, and connect with others in the dark, mysterious abyss of cyberspace.

Librarians today are finding it necessary to provide ever-increasing and varied services to patrons that they never see. Virtual reference in all types of libraries and support of distance education in academic institutions creates a whole new type of library user: the faceless patron. Library foot traffic is declining, but the expectations of libraries and librarians are constantly increasing. With libraries making the move more completely into this virtual environment, librarians are forced to wear many more hats: data miner, researcher, Internet and computer expert, multimedia specialist and webmaster, to name a few. "Librarians undergo constant training as new tools emerge. For many librarians, technological innovation is both stimulating and tiring . . . as a librarian, you can spend your whole life chasing technology."[1]

What is expected of librarians in the 21st century? It depends on whom you ask. The general public, when informed that professional librarians require a master's degree, usually respond with "I didn't know that you needed an advanced degree to shelve and check out books." However, human resources executives and presidents/CEOs of medium to large corporations are looking for "information specialist/librarians" who not only have advanced degrees, but significant and varied experience in information management. They are looking for highly trained and self-motivated professionals who can not only safeguard the company's precious proprietary information but can also assist and train employees on how to access the information they need to ensure the company is successful and profitable. Librarians are therefore faced with some public misconception of their jobs, while at the same time they continue struggling to provide the services that patrons, employers and the business community have begun not only to expect, but to *demand*—all of this in an environment of ever-diminishing budgetary resources and library staff.

Minimum expectations in the 21st century for a library professional? A master's degree, yes: be it a Master's of Library Science, a Master's of Library and Information Studies, a Master's of Science in Library Service, a Master's of Information Management and Library Science . . . there are too many variations to list, but you get the idea. The U.S. Department of Labor reports, "Most special librarians supplement their education with knowledge of the subject specialization, sometimes earning a master's, doctoral, or professional degree in the subject."[2]

How about experience in the 21st century? You betcha! Fallis and Fricke state, "Librarians need training in library skills, but it is not graduate-level education."[3] Employers would like to hire librarians with practical skills as well as theoretical knowledge. Since most library schools today do not focus on providing graduates with these practical skills, it is up to librarians to gain these skills through whatever means necessary: part-time employment, internships, additional course work (if available), and so on, before seeking a professional position.

So what exactly are we looking for in the librarian of the 21st century? Someone who is educated and experienced, obviously. Someone who's intelligent and resourceful, of course. Clearly, the level of expertise necessary will also depend on the area of specialty or the type of librarian that is being sought. Reference librarian, technical services librarian, electronic resources librarian, library administrator . . . they all do very different jobs. The one defining attribute of librarians today should be their ability, willingness, better yet, *drive* to do what librarians have done since the beginning of the profession: assist people in finding information and using it effectively. It seems pretty basic, doesn't it? Yet, there is so much involved in doing this seemingly simple thing and it gets more complicated every day.

Once again, we come back to the same question: What are we looking for in librarians today and for the 21st century? It's difficult to identify specific attributes that will apply in all situations. Generally, we need librarians who have prepared themselves through education and experience and have made an effort to keep abreast of new technological advances. We want librarians who are flexible, enthusiastic, have good stress management skills, are service oriented and have excellent interpersonal skills. And lastly we must have librarians who have that *drive* to learn and continue learning.

It seems pretty straightforward, doesn't it? Surprisingly, it isn't. To the astonishment of many, it really does take an exceptional person to enjoy working in a library and to become good at it. Even more importantly, it takes an extraordinary library worker to become a successful professional librarian in the 21st century.

NOTES

1. O. Crosby, "Information experts in the information age," *Occupational Outlook Quarterly* 44, no. 4 (2000): 3–15.

2. U.S. Department of Labor Bureau of Labor Statistics, *Occupational Outlook Handbook* (Indianapolis, IN: JIST Works, 2000).

3. D. Fallis, and M. Fricke, "Not by Library School Alone," *Library Journal* 124, no.16 (1999): 44–45.

13

Needed

Energetic Librarian Willing to Work in Challenging Arena!

Jetta Carol Culpepper

Criteria for employment as a librarian in the future will evolve and then change as rapidly as local management rewrites job descriptions. Changes will occur through efforts to achieve current goals and objectives supportive of the library's mission. These, too, will change. It seems fairly certain that the primary role of academic libraries will continually be that of support for the curriculum. A secondary activity will be to support faculty research. The third priority will be to facilitate the availability of the library as an option to others in the service community. The skills and knowledge held by successful candidates for jobs as academic librarians will surely support the library's primary purpose.

That is why search and screening committees for future academic librarians are seeking individuals who hold the master's degree from an American Library Association–accredited program as the minimum educational requirement. That degree will continue to endorse an expanding range of library and information science subject content. The curriculum will of necessity include computer skills and their library applications. A basic knowledge of library and information science will be replaced only by even stronger demands for updated learning. A second degree at the master's degree level, or above, will be required for tenure.

The new employee should not expect a mentor to fill gaps in preparation when classroom instruction is available. Two areas in which to seek additional preparation are the academic librarian's career and teaching. Simply being a library science student does not necessarily mean that one will gain knowledge of tenure, promotion, or the administrative systems of colleges and universities. Studying higher education will solve the problem. Librarians with faculty status can expect to be evaluated with the same criteria as that applicable to academic departmental faculty. Job performance, commitment to professional service, scholarly creativity, and the needs of the institution shall be considered. Positions where tenure is possible will emphasize skill in professional research and writing for publication.

In the second area, knowledge of teaching, training in teacher education and teaching experience are vitally important. Excellent teaching skills are required in presenting library instruction, guiding tours (including an introduction to library resources), and teaching research skills. Students and supervisors will evaluate this portion of the librarian's job performance. Criteria will be very similar to that applied in evaluating other teaching faculty at the institution of employment. Demands on future librarians will be stringent in the area of teaching, but a variety of responsibilities will mandate that the successful librarian be adaptable and/or amiable to change.

This profession is one of constant change. In applying professional learning such matters as cataloging rules and classification schedules for organizing information will continually change. Means of storing and making information available to customers will change with innovations in the commercial world. The library will gravitate toward providing resources and services resembling activities of an information broker. Consequently, organizational skills and time-management skills combined with talent in self-education will weigh more than can be predicted. Many jobs will require excellent oral, written, and interpersonal communication skills and the ability to work effectively in both a team-based environment and independently. In addition, managerial jobs will require effective leadership, and supervisory and managerial skills.

All criteria for employment will not be required for every job. Most jobs will concentrate on the application of specific skills. For example, people who excel in problem-solving and analytical skills will fill technically oriented jobs. All librarians will continually apply technology to a diverse range of matters from ordering and processing materials to service and business functions. Public service librarians may use technology in expanding outreach of the library to build stronger relations with faculty and students. Librarians beginning a career can anticipate moving about in the profession even if they stay in the same library throughout their career. Consequently, they will have opportunities to apply a variety of skills and different portions of their knowledge.

The professional with an ability to envision the library's role in the future and to anticipate the path may reach the cutting edge. On the other hand, given the time required for paperwork to travel through administrative channels, grants to be awarded, and/or institutional funding to be allocated, keeping up may be the goal. Hence, patience may be a characteristic of future librarians.

You ask, "What will search and screening committees look for in the 21st century?" The answer is somewhere in the above discussion and in the knowledge and skills required by yet unforeseen changes. Librarians are educators who perform in a challenging arena. Individuals who like their profession will hold an extensive knowledge of librarianship. They will be adaptable to a variety of responsibilities in combination with keeping an open mind toward learning, exhibit excellent customer-service skills, be adept with managerial and supervisory tasks, and maintain a motivated outlook combined with an energetic work style. Librarians will confidently face the challenges, use good judgment in handling the problems and work with a solid intent to meet research/information needs of clientele. Anticipate that job ads in the future will read, "Needed: Energetic Librarian Willing to Work in a Challenging Arena." Submit letter of interest with application items described in ad.

14

Wanted—New Creations
Dinosaurs Need Not Apply

Anne A. Salter

At a recent conference at an Ivy League campus library, I had an epiphany. Standing on an oriental carpet in the most beautiful of libraries surrounded by mahogany shelves filled with leather-bound volumes, I realized that I had stepped back into another world. For the first time in my career I felt that where I was and what I was viewing was not the library of the 21st century. I was viewing a dinosaur, albeit a very attractive one. The world of librarians is changing. If we do not realize this and change too, we, like the dinosaurs, will disappear. Do we want the new technology to be our Ice Age or our metamorphosis? Every profession has a time of evolution, a period of change in which the way it reaches its goals and fulfills its mission changes. These changes can be subtle or drastic depending on the catalyst. Our observation and response to this current period of evolution in our own profession is crucial to its well-being, success, and existence.

Our observation and response to technology over the last decades have successfully integrated into our traditions such watersheds as OCLC, the Internet, digitization, and electronic records. Our examination, experimentation and investigation of these have globally changed the face of libraries. The disappearance and replacement of the profession's icon—

the card catalog—reveals that we are collectively willing to experiment and make changes. We are courageous when it comes to equipment and process. We are less so when it comes to experimenting with our own self-awareness as professionals.

Over the last three decades we have seen technological innovations that we were willing to experiment with, adopt, and make an integral part of our practice. For example, OCLC not only changed the way we cataloged books and the speed by which are cataloged them, it created a unity in the profession. Additionally, it provided a link to and a standard for the archival profession. Its creation and implementation affected the way we did things and ultimately the way in which our patrons operated. Yet this same sense of experimentation and adaptation did not transfer into the basic curricula of our profession. Our inability to subjectively analyze our profession has resulted in the closing of library schools across the country, a dearth of trained professionals with library degrees, and an overall lack of identity. If we are to survive as a profession into the 21st century, it will be through a process of self-analysis. The willingness to experiment and risk change is crucial to the process.

It is time to admit that our professional preparation cannot continue through the simple addition of pertinent courses into existing curricula. By narrowing our trajectory, we have, in effect, programmed our own demise. We have failed to articulate a set of relevant standards that prepare a student with a library degree for entry into any profession except librarianship. Widening and broadening the concept of librarianship to prepare individuals for entry into a number of technology-based professions is long overdue. When it does occur, we lament the loss of our own to the high-tech, high-paying community. It is time to radically shift the way we envision our profession. Observation tells us that those library schools that are surviving are doing so because they elected to cooperate or combine with other disciplines. They either offer courses in information technology or have added classes in archival and records management. More changes are in order to meet the growing needs of our current evolution.

The librarian of the 21st century will be the product of what we observe about ourselves now and the critical self-analysis that follows. To begin this self-analysis, we must first articulate the traditions of our profession and the image that has resulted from those traditions. We must compare and contrast that image to the new one that is emerging. We must fully embrace the new technologies, allowing them to be our catalyst and not our eclipse. We must ask ourselves hard, deeply intense if not disturbing questions about our profession in order to fully understand and formulate our new image. Questions that challenge the following: our structure, leadership, missions, preparation for our roles, and our roles themselves.

A critical self-analysis will reveal those areas of the profession that are true cornerstones. It will equally reveal those areas that are a wasteland and require either total abandonment or complete overhaul. A few predictions are in order now. First, one of the major cornerstones of librarianship will be service. Exactly how, with what, or in what order and hierarchy remains to be seen. Another cornerstone is knowledge—globally, universal, transcending knowledge that includes technological know-how. A third is flexibility and includes flexibility in opening up our "guild" to outsiders who may or may not possess our traditional training. A final and fourth cornerstone is change. The future is mapped for major changes even now. Technology and its impact have just begun. Those who cannot see this and accept its impact are destined for the museum.

The librarian of the future is perhaps a professional who will no longer bear the name librarian. It is a professional who encompasses a set of standards and values that operate smoothly and seamlessly in a technology-driven environment. It is a professional who has a clear understanding of and appreciation for the traditions of librarianship. It is a professional who is multifaceted and multitasked. It is a professional with the characteristics of willingness to change; varied experience in training and background; adaptability to a quickly changing environment; "shareability" between disciplines; and commitment. It is, finally, a professional we will not recognize as a librarian in the usual sense. If we do, then we have failed to evolve.

15

Librarians

What Supervisors Are Seeking

Kathleen Fleming

In recent years, the need for public-service-oriented librarians has become increasingly important. In addition to housing books, journals, documents and other physical manifestations of the printed word, libraries are now places to go to accomplish the following tasks: access e-mail, send e-mail, access online journals or databases, fill out interlibrary loan forms to acquire a book or article from another library, obtain and photocopy course materials and acquire training for software applications. The library has become a process in addition to being a place.

A widely held belief is that because computers have become so important in our society, everyone knows how to use them. This is not true. Because libraries have always been places where people could go and be shown how to do something (use the card catalog, operate microfiche readers/printers, use microfilm readers and, in recent years, search the online catalog, photocopy, print), people naturally assume that a librarian can help them with all technological applications they may use. Patrons expect that a librarian will have all the necessary technical skills to provide assistance when something goes wrong with the sophisticated equipment present in almost all libraries. We provide more services now, and because patrons can do more at libraries now, more things can and do go wrong.

Librarians will always be asked to assist with problems patrons encounter while they are in the library, regardless of whether they are logical or appropriate (for example, what can a librarian do when a page from an online article prints a huge black smudge instead of the article text, or when a card for one of the many machines in the building gets stuck because two cards have been jammed into it?). Experienced librarians reading this essay are probably aware of these examples, so for these reasons, new hires must have a very strong public-service orientation. It also helps if they are technically savvy as well. And this means more than being able to program in JavaScript; it means new hires being able to think on their feet. We librarians cannot be afraid to explore and examine equipment in order to fix it.[1]

In addition to being able to locate elusive material, our job is to make people's library experience more productive and possibly more pleasant. In many libraries this means providing more nitty-gritty assistance. We often bristle at the "unprofessionalness" of some of this work (adding paper to copy machines or printers, using tweezers to get a paper jam out of a printer, using tweezers to pull a copy card out of a machine it was put into by accident), but it is really just part of our job. In the teaching profession, workshops are offered to allow teachers to develop the skill needed to resolve these types of problems and continuing education is a necessary component of every profession.

The most important quality of any librarian is a strong public-service orientation, and the willingness "to get your hands dirty" to resolve problems. This is followed closely by the realization that workshops and other forms of continuing education are another part of the job needed to keep skills current.

NOTE

1. Michael S. Houser, "Techno-wellness: Equipment working! Healthy climate! Happy teachers!" *Book Report* 19 (2001): 34–36.

16

Librarians and Human Interaction

Ronda Glikin

Beginning public service librarians learn very early in their career that going to library school did not prepare them enough to interact effectively with patrons at work. They find out that solving practical problems is something to learn on the job, not in a class.

Many years ago, when I got my degree, no classes in dealing with patrons on a day-to-day basis were either required of a graduate or even offered, and, today, the same situation is the norm. Why would librarians assume they should know intuitively how to handle whatever situations arise? We can take classes on computer instruction, systems theory, materials selection, and library administration, but where do we learn about human interaction? Can we sense when a patron is angry or fearful and why? Are we so intent on chasing new technologies that we ignore the value of establishing successful relationships with our patrons? What skills can we learn to help them feel more at ease? Taking counseling classes can be beneficial in a library public services setting.

It's time for a change!

Library schools need to offer classes on human relationships in order to fill a long-standing gap in library education. Such classes, essentially practical in nature, should teach such topics as:

1. Patron assumptions about librarians and libraries
2. Supporting patron strengths and downplaying weaknesses
3. Reading body language
4. Listening skills and effective ways of replying to patron questions
5. Ways of managing the complaining or angry patron for the best outcome
6. Best ways of making people with cultural differences or physical challenges feel they are being treated as well as other patrons, and
7. Creating an effective physical environment in the library (signage, placement of furniture and files, etc.).

Empathy, sympathy, patience, altruism, and the ability to listen are some of the required qualities of an effective public service librarian. The librarian needs to be able to make the patron feel at ease during the reference interview and bolster the patron's sense of self-confidence. After all, even short-term relationships can be complicated phenomena. It was not until I took a class in counseling skills in the early 1980s (after I had been a librarian for almost ten years) that I discovered I had needed to learn such skills in library school. As friendly and empathetic as I thought I was, I found that I still had a lot to learn.

Sara Fine in her article "Librarians and the Art of Helping," one of the few examples of an article relating library work to counseling skills, describes the benefits of applying counseling principles to library work. She provides examples of librarian-patron interactions and identifies underlying beliefs crucial to understanding the "real" problem. In addition to suggesting helpful responses, Fine gives examples of responses to be avoided and why, and she explains the elements involved in the counseling interview that everyone in the helping professions should be familiar with.

Public service librarians should be required to take a library class that teaches counseling skills in order to get their degree. Why not be prepared to defuse a serious situation or comfort an anxious patron *before* the situation arises, instead of (or in addition to) learning on the job? Maybe librarians who believe it is important to learn about the technology of a modern library should consider that it is at least equally as important to add the study of human relationships. In the future, librarians should be offered the option to do that.

REFERENCE

Fine, Sara. "Librarians and the Art of Helping." In *Philosophies of Reference Service,* edited by Celia Hales Mabry (Binghamton, NY: The Haworth Press, 1997).

17

A Business Plan Model of Employment for Librarians

Angela K. Horne

In the beginning of the 21st century, the financial fortunes of many startup companies faltered. The multimillion-dollar venture capital outlays of the 1990s to new and innovative firms either shrank in number or ceased entirely. High funding levels were replaced with high company failure rates. As stock prices plummeted, increasing numbers of staff lost their jobs, resulting in more and more office furnishings being liquidated on eBay. Aeron chairs were finally affordable for the rest of us.

Financial analysts have pointed to many reasons why the new economy hasn't met expectations. Among them is the weakness of many of these companies' business plans. A business plan should indicate to potential investors and business partners the company's objectives and future development path. It is significantly more than a slick PowerPoint presentation of vague prophecies, for it should take into consideration the market at large (and thus estimate the company's position in two years, in three years, in five years). However, rather than supply potential investors with realistic overviews of their business models, these failing startups masked their weak ideas with meaningless action statements and misguided financial predictions. In contrast, those companies whose officers craft strong, reliable business plans often rewrite them in response to changes in the market. A business plan is not a static document meant to exist for all time. Rather, it is a fluid reflection of a specific moment in a company's history. As the firm's strategies evolve, so too must its business model. The business plan reflects a company's market astuteness.

Historically, librarians often have been loath to adopt a business approach to their careers and workplaces. We rely on our strong service ethic and propensity to work for nonprofit organizations to shield us from market concerns. We have rarely considered the services offered by other libraries or private companies as completion with our own. We know that our work is invaluable, and that providing access to information is a worthy lifelong pursuit; how could others not as well? Many within our profession are only beginning to realize that our activities will benefit from being cast in the framework of a business model. By identifying our areas of expertise and planning for the future, we will be able to position ourselves with a flexibility similar to that of the most astute business executives. This is particularly true of librarians seeking employment in the modern library.

Business plans already occur in several library contexts. A library applicant's résumé could be considered his or her personal business plan. Within such categories as "experience," "education," "goals" and "special skills," she or he indicates why a prospective employer should invest in one candidate and not another. In preparing their personal business plan, candidates reflect on their core qualities and career goals, fashioning a plan that will aid their climb up the librarianship ladder. Their investors (the library administration) must be convinced that a particular plan is the best match for the open position. What indicators of the candidate's potential does the plan provide? How has the candidate indicated that he or she will be more successful in the position than any other? A well-developed résumé is required to open the interviewer's door.

Alternatively, the applicant should be familiar with the hiring library's business plan. Though the library will likely use other words to describe this document, it does exist, and may consist of several items. These include its mission statement, annual report, and related planning materials. All of these documents are invaluable resources for the candidate, for they reveal whether the library has clearly identifiable objectives. Questions the candidate should be able to answer after perusing these materials are the same ones an investor would ask of a fledgling firm in search of funding. What is the library's strategic outlook? What are its organizational values? Does it have a plan in place to respond to market demands? How are services and products marketed to patrons? Candidates should pay especial attention to the hiring library's commitment to re-envisioning itself; is it an agile, evolving organization? Many of the companies whose business plans failed them during the past several months were the victims of shortsightedness and inability to develop full responses to such questions. So too can weak explanatory materials undermine the library's activities.

A representative document for overall library initiatives is the Cornell University Library Digital Futures Plan. It provides potential employees with a blueprint of not only our future development goals but also those already accomplished. It is amended annually, to reflect the progress under each planning point, and is a key document for the entire library system. Staff refer to it frequently, as do individuals external to the library. It serves as a reminder of our vision for the library's future, its collections, staff, and services. Reading the similar plan for one's preferred place of employment is key to understanding how the new employee would help achieve the institution's goals. Does the candidate's résumé reflect core competencies or work experience desired by the hiring library?

Familiarity with the creation of business plans benefits all parties to the library employment process. The ability to pitch convincingly one's talents is a true skill. Just as entrepreneurs in search of funding descend on venture capital fairs with clearly worded business plans in hand, hopeful library employees send their personal business plans to human resources offices and await interviews. If employers and employees examine each other's "business plan" carefully, and pose probing follow-up questions about the details of such documents, then the most suitable candidates may be hired for open positions. Let us avoid the unwanted scenario of investments in staff who are not true matches for the organization.

18

Hot Links Are Hot Hires

Virginia E. Young

The most exciting Web pages are ones with lots of links, not just straight text. Links tempt the user down multiple paths, exploring unforeseen options. I want my librarians to be links, not just words. They should be able to make new, spontaneous connections both with the staff within the library and with our patrons in the college.

Our library serves a small, four-year, liberal arts college. As the director of the library, I have four professional positions with which to cover all the usual services. When I fill a vacancy, there is no position, for example, where the candidate can choose to catalog monographs only. The only option is to be multi-tasking: catalog monographs and videos, liaise with a department, and work a few hours on the reference desk. My librarians are involved in the whole library.

Thus I need people who see bridges, not islands, within the library. It's easy to separate out technical functions and put those people in the back room, and to allow only public service people to staff public service desks. I need someone who sees how to link staff from different areas of the library to allow materials to flow into the system and out with the patron. Personnel aren't *your* people versus *my* people; we are *our* people.

On the other hand, I need a bridge from the library out to the patron. The library has shifted its paradigm of the medieval treasure house to that of the network hub. The paradigm for librarians changes apace. No longer are librarians seen as guardians and gatekeepers, ensconced in their ivory palaces, but they are swept by market demands into the flow of the Internet. Now they are marketers of library resources and publicity-savvy.

Library patrons push and pull this new paradigm. Faculty without current technology skills need the librarian to help them learn the electronic resources. Students at ease with the latest computer program need a librarian who helps them evaluate what they find. Either way, the librarian has to see new ways of searching for, evaluating and using information, and communicating this knowledge to patrons.

Casual conversations before a committee meeting starts, a chance encounter on the sidewalk in front of the dining hall, or at lunch itself, may be the catalyst for scheduling a BI class, or highlighting a new resource. But serendipitous meetings don't happen when a librarian stays in her office in the library. This does not call for pushiness, merely a readiness to see possibilities and then to act. What other ways are there for making a hot link in the patron's mind to a resource in the library?

This shift in the heart of a librarian's work affects what is valued and sought in a candidate. No longer is in-depth knowledge of traditional print resources invaluable; the ability to learn and keep up with new search engines may be the key to a successful librarian. Perhaps managerial experience in another service industry will move an application to the interview list. An outgoing personality will win over one that prefers solitary work at the computer. An eagerness to teach and to share will be a desirable qualification.

Candidates for a position in my library may have specialized in one area during library school, or in their first job at a large institution. That's great, but I need people who can see where they could branch out. I need people who like going to workshops, pre-conferences, and institutes. I don't mind funding the learning; I just need people willing to learn.

This is reflected in our job ads. At the moment, our search committees work with small pools of candidates. We don't have a long list of required qualifications; we will be lucky to hire at all. Instead of seeking a specialized professional, we might admire a talented person with a new degree who is eager to try on the whole profession. We're a great place to work if you are unsure about what you want to do in a library. Here you can sample a little of everything! It's an excellent chance for a new librarian to try out several aspects of librarianship, or for experienced librarians who don't like to be too narrowly channeled in their job.

So I look for a candidate who is not only excited by the possibility of working within the whole library, but has a personality that reaches out to people to make connections. It's like those hot links on Web pages. I want to hire someone who will hot link our library.

19

Technology Skills in Libraries of the 21st Century

Sheila Kasperek

Computer technologies are becoming a part of many library jobs and as we progress into the 21st century, the role of technology in information services will expand. What technology will become standard or adopted by a particular institution or library is anybody's guess, but what is certain is that developing good computer skills is essential for the librarian of the future.

Just a few short years ago the Internet blossomed and many libraries began developing Web pages to organize and publicize internal and external links to information. While some libraries developed simple pages listing hours and locations, others have developed complex pages using a wide variety of languages. North Carolina State University libraries offer customized Web layouts called "My Library."[1] The Pasadena Public Library website has a Web tutorial written in HTML and ASP. California State University, Fullerton library offers online video tours of its library.

These are just a few examples of what is currently happening with library websites. A review of recent job postings listed a veritable alphabet soup of required and preferred computer skills. Just a short time ago PERL was the hot new Web programming language. Now ASP and PHP are showing themselves as the language of the day. Looking at job descriptions for Web-savvy librarians could include a mix or match of any of the following skills: HTML, XML, SMIL, PERL, PHP, ASP, SQL, JSP, JavaScript, Cold Fusion, Java, Dreamweaver, Flash, and Visual Basic. This is in addition to non-Web technologies, including Microsoft Word, Excel, Access, PowerPoint, and numerous desktop publishing programs.

This lengthy list of skills can seem daunting and leave a job-seeking librarian wondering which technologies to spend the time learning and in how much depth. Many organizations have already adopted specific software and languages that they support, and what is supported by one institution may or may not be supported by another. If you are already in an organization, you should determine what options you have before investing time learning a language or program, but if you are in the market for a new position, the question remains, what to learn?

HTML is a good base level of skill. While more dynamic languages develop, HTML is, and will remain for some time, the standard. It will be accepted everywhere for many years to come as it is the language that opened the Internet to the individual. Learn HTML, beyond what WYSIWYG editors like Microsoft FrontPage and Netscape Composer offer. HTML is easy to learn and is required before you can build any Web programming skills into your repertoire. Soon, HTML will become a basic skill for many jobs, both in and out of libraries.

Beyond HTML, this is where some variation and personality can come into play. While you could learn a little bit about each language, a person looking for a technology position would be better off to invest the time in learning one or two languages and/or programs well. Developing depth of knowledge in one or two areas demonstrates the ability to learn something and learn it well. So learn a new skill, complete some projects to show off those skills especially if they are library-related, and use these projects to sell your skills. Show that you are adaptable, confident in your abilities and proud of your work.

Most positions, library and otherwise, list both required and preferred skills. Some institutions mean what they say when they say "required." They refuse to review applicants who do not meet the "requirements," and if no successful applicant is found, they must advertise again with a different list of requirements rather than review existing nonqualified applicants. Others are not as strict. If an appropriate applicant is not found, they will review applications that do not meet the requirements. Since you can't be sure what the hiring rules of an institution are, apply for the position you are interested in, tout any related skills and then buckle down and learn the required skills. Not only will you meet the job requirements

20

A Word to Future Academic Librarians

Vickie Kline

If you've looked at recent job ads for academic librarians, you've probably noticed that most have daunting checklists of requirements. When you factor in "preferred" technical skills, some of the job descriptions are enough to scare those of us already in the field into early retirement. I agree that having a prodigious arsenal of skills is of great value, but there are other factors to consider while preparing for a career as an academic librarian. I believe we must think hard about which beliefs and character traits will most benefit us as we serve our students and institutions.

If I had to pick a single, overriding trait as an asset for future academic librarians, it would be an unshakeable commitment to teaching information literacy skills. Our students face an information landscape that is radically different from the sheltered havens that we experienced as students. We worked with finite collections of carefully selected materials. By contrast, our students will work in electronic environments where the boundaries between scholarly information, popular resources, and outright misinformation are blurred. As traditional resources migrate to online formats, it will become more and more difficult for students to find and evaluate information effectively.

Helping our students do battle in this chaotic information arena must be our top priority as librarians. We need to teach students how to search effectively in this new environment. When students find unanchored bits of information, they must be motivated to place them in context and to evaluate them with care. Most importantly, we need to persuade them that the extra time and hard work is well spent.

We, as librarians, need to develop a different sort of literacy—student literacy! Student literacy will help us understand how students approach research. An idealistic desire to encourage effective research skills must be grounded in a realistic understanding of typical student motivations and information-seeking habits. Our students are often one click, or page, away from abandoning quality resources for easier paths. If we don't keep this fact constantly in mind, we cannot even begin to meet their needs.

Moreover, we can't assume that students will come into the library and place themselves in our tender care. Some students will only know us through the electronic services we provide. We must fight vigilantly for systems and tools that make it easier for students to find high-quality academic resources. Hopefully, through these systems, we can artfully enlighten students about information along the way. If all else fails, we have to find ideal, intriguing information sources and place them where reluctant researchers can't help but trip over them.

Do these seem like overwhelming challenges for even devoted acolytes of information literacy? They are! Here are a few short comments on fundamental personality traits that will make these tasks seem easier:

Curiosity—If you are content within the boundaries of the world you know now, you will never learn what is possible. Learning about an ever-changing information world is much more fun when you genuinely enjoy exploring!

Intuition—Many services or tools might not look like much at first glance. Keep a sharp eye out for those ideas with long-range potential.

Energy and endurance—Expect that you will be working on the very edge of change throughout your career. It doesn't get easier. Find ways to keep your energy flowing!

Comfort with chaos—Change is the only constant. Be happy if you can predict even 20 percent of what happens. Plans are moving targets, not commandments set in stone.

Humor—A sense of humor helps you deal with the unexpected. It also proves to students and co-workers that you are a human being!

Service—Your primary goal is helping students. Don't lose sight of this when you're tinkering with services and systems. Focus on the resources that the students need and any tools that can make research clearer or easier. If students ultimately don't find what they need, you share the responsibility.

Being a librarian in the next few decades won't be an easy task. A lot of folks believe we can't adapt fast enough to keep up with new information technologies. If we remember that we're fighting for our students, and not just ourselves, I believe we can. As someone near and dear to me would say, "It's time to hang tough!"

21

Preferred Qualification
Ability to Think Conceptually

Melinda Dermody

Under "Qualifications" in some job descriptions, you may find that a library is seeking an individual who is an "innovative" or "forward" thinker. In the most limited way, this could be defined as someone who is able to deal with the rapidly changing environment of libraries today. Taken in another sense, it means someone who is able to think about library service in ways that expand beyond any specific job skills or experience. It is from these types of "thinkers" that exciting and creatively enhanced services are developed in libraries. As much as specific skills are important in a job, so is the ability to think and consider these skills in expanded ways.

In library school, we learn a variety of things that are necessary for being good librarians. We are trained on how to work in specific areas of the library. For example, we may learn about how to be a reference librarian, how to provide reference service and how to use important reference sources. We may not, however, learn how to think about the larger idea of what it means to "provide" reference service to our patrons. Graduates entering an area such as reference will do a better job if they are able to think about how the specific skills they learned in school fit into these important, larger concepts. The 24/7 online reference desk, for instance, is an idea that came from individuals who were able and willing to think expansively about what "providing" service could mean.

Another area to consider is instruction. In order to train instruction librarians, library schools often offer courses on teaching, and becoming an instruction librarian. In most academic libraries, however, an educational mission underlies nearly all services in the library, from reference to circulation. Instruction does not stop outside the door of the academic library's classroom or lab. The training of instruction librarian skills may not be sufficient to develop an educational philosophy that is able to run through all aspects of the library. Broad thinking about education can shape instructional services in such creative ways as webcasting a library instruction session. Broad thinking can also underlie traditionally noninstructional undertakings, such as Web page development. There is an educational element, for example, in many innovative endeavors such as the development of Web portals for a library's website, or the creation of extensive metadata for resources.

Of course technology, and its use in all areas of the library, is a large part of what we encounter during graduate school. We learn how to do sophisticated searches in databases, create Web pages, and provide access to electronic resources. With all of these services, the idea of "access" is important. How would library services further develop if, for instance, librarians thought about access in terms of "access to everything, everywhere, all the time" when evaluating or implementing new ideas? With broad thinking, we would give imaginative considerations to technological opportunities, enhancements of service desks, and maybe even the building itself. It is this type of thought that allowed libraries to determine that digitizing a video or music recording and putting it on electronic reserve is an excellent way to provide patrons with access to what they need, when and where they need it.

With new and experienced librarians thinking about library services in conceptual and expansive ways, enhanced and innovative new services are likely to flourish. Additionally, broader thinking also allows librarians to put their specific responsibilities into a context that may be more meaningful to them professionally. Interlibrary loan librarians struggling with the technological details of how to e-mail periodical articles directly to their patrons may, for example, recognize that their individual skills and efforts are part of the library's larger commitment to provide excellent, out-reaching service and resources to patrons.

I encourage library school graduates, before they enter the profession, to briefly step back from their recently acquired skills to think about how these skills fit into a broader, more conceptual scheme of library service.

Of course, this understanding will increase with work experience, but it may also help when nervously sitting in an interview, you are suddenly asked something like, "In what direction do you see library services developing?" You will find yourself prepared to answer more than such questions as 1), why are you interested in this job? or 2), what experience do you have teaching? Thinking conceptually about library services could not only get you the job, but also benefit the library that hires you, and enhance library services in the long run.

22

Voices from the 21st Century

Librarians at the University of Arizona Library

Carla J. Stoffle, Patricia Morris, and Ninfa Trejo

Ten years ago, the University of Arizona librarians asked, "If we are to be successful in the 21st century, what should we be doing and how should we be organizing our work?" By talking to our users and examining our workflow, we came to understand that the primary focus for determining this must be our customers and their needs, with customer satisfaction the major measure of our success. At the same time, our librarians determined that the values underlying our work and our decisions about our work must remain those associated specifically with librarianship; for example, information as a public good, equity of access regardless of ability to pay, individual privacy, diversity, information literacy education, empowering users to be self-sufficient, and maintenance of an environment conducive to intellectual freedom.

As a result of eighteen months of review, the organizational structure of the library was flattened into functional teams organized to reflect the university's structure, with an overlapping set of cross-functional teams to perform specific activities or design and implement strategic goals. The purpose of this structure was to maximize staff resources, knowledge and skills, as well as stimulate greater creativity and problem-solving abilities among our staff. Another outgrowth of the restructuring was a reconceptualization of the position descriptions for librarians specifying that, in general, librarians would engage in assessment, collection management, in-depth information provision, education activities from information literacy to copyright and information policy issues, knowledge management from organizing all types of information regardless of format to engaging in the creation of new knowledge products and electronic publishing, and connection development. The work of librarians was set in the same context as the expectations for all the other library employees. This was accomplished by including the values adopted specifically by the University of Arizona in each librarian's position description.

All staff are charged with advancing the mission and vision of the library through system-wide thinking and shared responsibility for successful teams. Individuals are responsible and accountable for problem solving and process improvement and are empowered to make decisions at appropriate levels. Staff are encouraged to take satisfaction in their accomplishments in an atmosphere of cooperation and to have balanced personal and professional lives that reflect the following values:

- Continuous improvement and learning—we strive to exceed our expectations, raise our standards and challenge ourselves.
- Diversity—We value, respect and are strengthened by viewpoints and experiences outside the dominant culture. We strive to build a multicultural organization.
- Customer focus—We actively seek to identify, meet and exceed customer wants and needs. We welcome, guide and support customers with attention and respect. We create and sustain partnerships. We provide access to information in its most useful form.
- Integrity—We honor our commitments by doing what we say we will do. We hold ourselves and each other accountable and behave in a consistently ethical and responsible manner.
- Flexibility—We respect varying approaches to problem solving and meeting customer needs. We value and support collaboration, teamwork and other creative methods as a basis for making decisions and developing programs.

Of course, this new environment has had its challenges. When do librarians wear their specialist as opposed to their generalist hats? How do they prioritize their many projects and best use their time in an environment where there is not enough time? How do we recognize and demonstrate appreciation for librarians who have had a long-standing commitment to the institution, while sharing leadership with less senior librarians and staff as they emerge as the appropriate choice for an assignment? Most of this requires a constant openness to questioning—from each of us, including the dean. As a dean it has become imperative I give up control and decision-making as prescribed by our understandings, providing a model for others as well as facilitating the functioning of a team organization. That is why, for this paper, I have decided to work with two librarians, librarians who are clearly grounded in the 21st century. I asked them their perspectives on the topic I was asked to address, librarians for the 21st century, and more specifically what it means to be a 21st-century librarian at the University of Arizona Library.

Patricia Morris is an associate librarian for the Science and Engineering Team. When asked why she selected this library for employment seven years ago, she reflected that:

"My first impression of the University of Arizona Libraries after my onsite interview could be summed up in two phrases, limitless innovative opportunities and flexible supportive infrastructure. For me this meant that, at least in theory, this was a place where it would be hard not to succeed. The potential for challenges and growth and the opportunity to develop as a 'leading-edge' thinker were there.

"Of course, reality soon set in. Things are not static; everything is always changing and evolving here. Now I understand that I must utilize creative ambiguity as a constructive tool. My greatest challenge, therefore, is to exist in a continuous process improvement state of mind as I plan, create and analyze the services I provide to customers."

Asked to identify one incident that identifies her 21st-century librarian role, Patricia told her "SPARC" story. As the librarian serving the department of Ecology and Evolutionary Biology, Patricia took the opportunity to work with a faculty member who expressed his frustration at what he saw as the arbitrary price increases for scientific journals instituted by commercial publishers. He knew what he was talking about, as the journal he edited had increased its price 300 percent in less than a five-year span. Patricia described to this faculty member the new initiative by the Association of Research Libraries, SPARC (Scholarly Publishing and Academic Resources Coalition). Thus began an important coalition. As a result of this collaboration, a new journal, *Evolutionary Ecology Review,* is in the marketplace at a fair cost. It is a genuine competitor to its commercially published counterpart as reflected by its distinguished editorial board, important scholarly content and timely publication schedule. Michael Rosenzweig, the faculty member involved, has also become a crusader on and off campus about the value of librarians to improving the scholarly communication process. Patricia has had an important national as well as local impact.

Ninfa Trejo is a Social Sciences librarian who works with the Mexican American Studies and Psychology departments. Why does she value librarianship, especially as it manifests itself during this 21st century and at the University of Arizona Library?

"I know that this library will continue to use the core values of librarianship as it faces the decisions of the 21st century. For me, the use of the Pueblo storyteller as our symbol embodies this commitment—a commitment to storytelling by providing essential information for learning as well as transmitting cultural knowledge. At the same time, we are preparing for the future by our commitment to continual learning and improvement that will develop our individual strengths and will assist us in responding to the changing needs of our customers. I also value the learning that enables me to gather data and use systems thinking to set my priorities and to participate in our shared decision-making environment. I have learned that it is important to develop one's strengths and feel comfortable in taking risks. During my second year, I knew that I needed to acquire a more sophisticated teaching methodology and to study pedagogical principles to improve my instruction and my technological skills. Knowing this, I worked with peers on a plan for learning, applying my learning and being accountable. Now I am comfortable with my education responsibilities and my peers share with me that I am much more effective. This constructive honest feedback process has been invaluable. Personally, it is important that in my work and scholarship I address the gap between the information rich and the information poor. Equity of access and promotion of diversity are core values for me—ones that I get to address in my daily work in this library. I feel that I am making a difference in the education of all of our students with the programs I get to implement that increase cultural awareness and enhance understanding of cultural diversity. Where else are you expected to bring your values with you and allows you to implement them in your everyday work?"

As Patricia and Ninfa exemplify, librarians have the opportunity to make unique contributions in this changing environment of academic libraries and higher education. Those who are committed to excellence and who want choice, opportunities for creativity and responsibility within the context of a customer-centered and values-driven organization will flourish anywhere. We insist upon these characteristics as the entry qualifications for our librarians at the University of Arizona Library.

23

Being a Deep Generalist

Leslie M. Haas

I think back to my library school days and there are so many things I wish someone had told me about what it means to be an academic librarian in the 21st century. We learned a lot of theory, we studied Dewey and cataloging, learned how to conduct a reference interview and how to write a collection development policy. What they did not teach us is how to deal with constant change, the politics of the library, staff versus librarians, faculty status: what does it really mean? Many of us learned this on the job(s) and had experienced librarians teach us the ropes. As head of a reference department in an academic institution, I want to pass this advice along to you as you think about what you want to do with your degree:

1. Be a "deep generalist." This means continue to learn about resources and patron needs outside your area of specialization. To be a good reference librarian in today's academic library, you need to be able to answer questions about all sorts of topics and even if you work at a specialized library, the patron does not always ask questions related just to that topic.[1]

2. Learn how to market yourself. This is not taught in library school, but you need to know how to sell yourself and your skills not just to your

future employer, but to the constituency you have been hired to serve. This means getting out and introducing yourself to faculty, staff and students; giving away pens or magnets with your name on it; and getting your homepage placed prominently on a departmental Web page. In other words, make them aware of what you can offer them and be proactive in getting them what they need. For example, download a copy of a faculty member's syllabus and vita and send them alerts or articles that may help them with either their teaching or research needs.[2]

3. Faculty status: yes or no? Faculty status has long been debated in academic circles and everyone has an opinion about what the status really means. As you interview for a job in academia, ask about faculty status and find out what it means at that particular institution. There are no two universities that operate the same way and you need to make sure you are comfortable with the policies and procedures outlined in the library's policy. You should also find out about the process; how many librarians have not received tenure; is there a post-continuing review once tenure is granted; what kind of release time is offered so you can do research and write articles; how does promotion work? You should also find out if the decision about retention goes outside the library; in other words, is there a faculty committee that reviews all faculty and votes on whether to accept you into the ranks?[3]

4. Constant change. You have probably heard from professors about how fast things are changing, and if you have any prior experience in libraries, you already know how fast libraries are changing. You should be honest with yourself about how comfortable you are with change and also recognize that your job will change in ways that will not always be reflected in your job description. Be prepared to be a lifelong learner.[4]

There are so many things today's librarian needs to know and I could go on and on about so many topics, but I will stop right here. The final piece of advice that I have is to have fun and enjoy what you do.[5]

NOTES

1. Available online at: http://www.lib.ncsu.edu.

2. Available online at: http://www.mnsfld.edu/depts/lib.

3. Available online at: http://www.library.fullerton.edu/tour.

4. American Libraries job postings from January–May 2001, and positions posted on different websites for same dates.

5. Joshua Marpet, "If Adaptability Has Made You a Generalist, Learn How to Pitch It and Get Hired," *InfoWorld* 22 (24 April 2000): 100.

REFERENCES

Albrecht, Karl. "The True Information Survival Skills." *Training & Development* 55 (February 2001): 24–30.

Jeffery, R. Brooks. "Librarians as Generalists: Redefining Our Role in a New Paradigm." *Art Documentation* 17 (1998): 25–29.

Marpet, Joshua. "If Adaptability Has Made You a Generalist, Learn How to Pitch It and Get Hired." *InfoWorld* 22 (24 April 2000): 100.

24

Academic Reference Librarians for the 21st Century

Colleen Boff and Carol Singer

In 1990, *Library Personnel News* asked several leaders of the American Library Association to predict what a librarian's job might be in the year 2000. One such prediction was that the trend toward CD-ROM and optical media would continue.[1] Although it is obviously risky to predict the future, one common prediction is that change is inevitable.

In their introduction to *Creating the Agile Library,* Haricombe and Lusher wrote, "It is often said that change is the only constant. This change is all around us, and the rate at which it occurs is faster than ever before. As we approach the end of the twentieth century, few can dispute that a large measure of the transformations are the result of advances in technology. With its ever-present drive for faster and better ways to process and disseminate information, technology is fueling changes in society at large and in academia especially."[2] In their book, they suggest developing agile libraries to respond to all this change. They define an agile library as a user-centered library that "permits the flexibility to take risks to make responsive changes that will address its users' needs."[3]

Agile libraries will, of course, require agile librarians. What would an agile academic reference librarian look like? He or she must be willing and able to assess and alter the reference area, the collections, policies, methods, attitudes, or anything else in order to offer the most effective and appropriate service possible. Although this type of librarian is user-centered rather than library-centered, an agile librarian would not be a radical departure from the past.

In some ways, the characteristics of a successful academic reference librarian are the same today as they were years ago. Reference librarians must have a broad knowledge of paper and electronic sources and the ability to instantly choose the best, most appropriate sources and formats to answer each question. Traditional skills, such as the ability to conduct reference interviews, are more important than ever, with librarians doing reference in person, by telephone, by e-mail, Internet chat, or Web contact center software. The use of computers has resulted in the need for reference librarians to keep their technological skills sharp in addition to being experts at these more conventional skills.

Above all, an academic reference librarian must have a willingness, even an eagerness, to learn new skills, new sources and new attitudes. The new reference librarian must be ready to commit to a lifetime of continuing education and to searching for ways to improve the skills and knowledge he or she brings to the job. Continuing education can include several approaches, such as attending professional conferences and workshops or taking additional classes. It can include reading professional journals and books or subscribing to one or more of the many e-mail discussion lists that are so valuable for staying current in the profession. There are also a multitude of Internet sites that provide useful information for librarians. Staying current is a constant struggle, but the effort to do so must become a habit.

No longer is it enough for librarians to continuously update their skills and knowledge, they must also find innovative ways to promote library services and resources. Many librarians feel they are competing with the increasingly popular "expert" services on the Web, such as Askanexpert, Askme, Webhelp or Inforocket, and natural language search engines such as Ask Jeeves. These services may be one reason for the drop in the number of reference queries reported by the Association of Research Libraries.[4] We can no longer assume that our users will think of the library as the primary place to find information. Geordano et al. wrote, "Paradoxically, the librarians discovered that the more they embraced technology, the less relevant the library was in the eyes of the students."[5] While it is important for librarians to stay abreast of technological advances, it is crucial that they are proactive in promoting their services and resources as well as educating their constituents.

The ideal person who should consider becoming an academic reference librarian in the 21st century is one who is not afraid of constant change, embraces learning something new every day of his or her life, enjoys the challenge of problem solving and is one who can think beyond boundaries. We are and will always be a service profession regardless of the medium in which we communicate to others. Not only will the librarians of the 21st century need to be masters of the art of librarianship, they will also need to be master learners, communicators, educators, and changemasters.

NOTES

1. "The Librarian's Job of the Future," *Library Personnel News* 4, no. 2 (Spring 1990): 18–19.

2. Lorraine J. Haricombe and T.J. Lusher, eds., *Creating the Agile Library: A Management Guide for Librarians* (Westport, CT: Greenwood Press, 1998), xii.

3. Ibid., xiv.

4. Roy Tennant, "Determining Our Digital Destiny," *American Libraries* 31, no. 1 (January 2000): 54–55.

5. Peter Geordano, Christine Menard, and Rebecca Ohm Spencer, "The Disappearing Reference Desk," *College & Research Libraries News* 62, no. 7 (July/August 2001): 692.

25

"The More Things Change"

What Is a Librarian Today?

Cynthia Akers

There is a well-known quotation by Alphonse Karr, a French novelist and journalist, that translates as "The more things change, the more they remain the same." As a practicing reference librarian of the 21st century, of course, I double-checked the wording of the quotation in a standard source. My source, though, was the website Bartleby.com, which allowed me to search in its "Reference" category such titles as the 2001 *Columbia Encyclopedia*, the 2001 *American Heritage Dictionary of the English Language*, and the 1996 *Columbia World of Quotations*. A few keywords and fewer seconds later, I had my verification and a beginning to this essay.[1]

It is certainly not fresh news that technology has changed drastically our access to information sources in reference service. For instance, as I write this essay at our reference desk in an academic library, I am watching our patrons seemingly mesmerized by our banks of computers. Between sentences, I answer questions about locating articles in full text (and dealing with patrons' disappointment when I say, "No, that article isn't available electronically—but you can find it in our Periodicals department on microfilm").

I also serve as an adjunct faculty member of Emporia State University's School of Library and Information Management. Often in my courses, I tell students that my daily work as a reference librarian has evolved greatly over the years from my first professional library position in 1988. And, that evolution is true in terms of the electronic sources I consult, the way I communicate with staff and patrons via e-mail, and the sheer dependence I have upon my desktop computer for my routine activities.

However, I also discuss with these students their roles as future information professionals. A question I pose in one course is, "In this age of technology, do librarians matter?" A simple and obvious answer is "Yes—we do matter." The more complex answer, though, is "Yes—but how do we convince the world that we matter?" Anne Grodzins Lipow, in an article titled "Reference Service in a Digital Age," notes that ". . . reference service didn't always exist. Of the four major functions we take for granted in libraries today—collecting quality materials for a particular constituency, organizing those materials on the shelves and creating public records so they can be found directly by the user, circulating those materials, and helping the individual users who can't help themselves—the last (reference service) is, in fact, a relatively recent development. Over-the-counter reference didn't surface until the late 1800s, and when it finally occurred it was despite the protests of numerous librarians who thought that such a service was highly presumptuous and inappropriate."[2]

It is interesting to look back on this long-ago need to justify reference service during this time of global, instantaneous electronic information transfer. Today, Internet sites such as Questia and the Electric Library pride themselves on marketing directly to consumers and stating that all research needs can be met by their services.

What, then, can librarians provide and what has *not* changed in an age of technology? I believe that a newly minted MLS graduate needs to possess certain characteristics for the profession today:

Flexibility. I noted earlier that my role in reference has evolved already and will continue to evolve. An entry-level librarian should, if possible, look for a position that will offer opportunities for this flexibility. Even if the position does not specify such responsibilities as Web page creation, library instruction, or subject-specific collection development, these responsibilities are increasingly in demand and a new person to the profession will most likely be asked to step into one or more of these requirements. In addition, library organizations are likely to be transformed as the mission of that library changes to serve developing clienteles. If we see ourselves as only performing one job and no others, we may find that there is no place for us in a reorganization.

Curiosity. The field of information transfer has created exciting prospects for virtual reference service for patrons worldwide, as well as expanded availability of electronic books, journals, and unique Internet sources for a range of general and esoteric subjects. However, these resources serve no purpose without the willingness of information professionals to explore, learn, and teach the retrieval and evaluation of this information to their patrons. We must remain enthusiastic and interested about not only the practice of information retrieval, but also the creation of this knowledge itself—in other words, keeping intellectual curiosity alive.

Questioning. Brenda Dervin and Patricia Dewdney in "Neutral Questioning: A New Approach to the Reference Interview" outline the concepts of *open, closed,* and *neutral* questioning in eliciting the patron's actual information need. Open questions "allow users to respond in their own words. . . . [they] are invitations to talk" about the explicit or implicit information request at hand.[3] Closed questions invite yes or no answers and serve as useful closers to the reference interview, given that they also "involve a judgment already made by the librarian of what is relevant to the user." Neutral questions such as "What would you like to know about this topic?" address the elements of information situations, gaps in knowledge, and/or the potential uses of the information to be found. While this description of open, closed, and neutral questioning is necessarily brief, it should be emphasized that methods of questioning do not change with the advent of technology. Listening to the question, rephrasing the information need, and following up to learn if the need has been met can and should be accomplished not only in person, but also via e-mail, chat, discussion forums, and any other means of virtual/digital reference service. The new information professional who possesses questioning skills will succeed in any position.

And yes, I am an information professional—but I am, and will continue to be, a librarian. The term expresses my continued love for the structure of a library and for my profession itself. I hope that new people in our field will feel the same way.

NOTES

1. Columbia world of quotations (1996). Retrieved August 18, 2001, from http://www.bartleby.com.
2. A.G. Lipow, "Reference service in a digital age," *Reference and User Services Quarterly* 38 (1998): 47–81.
3. Dervin and Dewdney, 509.

26

Reference Staff of the Digital Beyond

Beth Avery

In a time where change is pervasive, it is no surprise that the tools used by librarians to answer patrons' questions, and even the kinds of questions and the way their patrons ask are constantly changing. However, the basic mission to provide excellent information services to our users will not change. The traditional role of teacher and guide will continue and will become even more important as the quantity of information increases and the quality varies even more widely. While it is no easy task to imagine what reference service will look like in the next decade, we can be sure that the increased use of technology will emphasize the importance of the library staff itself over the physical location of information. Therefore, the success of our services must continue to be built on our human assets.

The qualifications needed for the librarian who is able to provide effective and efficient service in this changing world are also changing. In the past we have placed the emphasis on knowledge, skills and abilities. Looking at current job advertisements, one sees an increasing emphasis on attitudes, such as "willingness to embrace change," "flexibility," "enthusiastic." As the structure of reference work changes, increased emphasis is placed on staff who can evolve and grow into new (perhaps as yet undefined) positions as the needs of the libraries' patrons change.

This does not mean we won't look for skills and abilities. What we will look for are competencies in overall areas, rather than specific skills. So rather than knowledge of a specific reference tool, we will seek librarians who can understand and effectively apply new technologies. In order to do this, they will need to be able to analyze and be sensitive to user needs. We need those risk takers who are skeptical enough to honestly evaluate the usefulness of new technologies and methods of information delivery to meet the needs of our users and libraries.

With wider acceptance and use of 24/7 online reference services, there will be fewer in-person interactions. The emphasis won't be on local collections, but on technology-mediated access to information regardless of location. As a result, methods of communication will change and, to some, may appear to be reverting to early times when concise written communication was necessary. However, the big difference will be the librarians' ability to multitask. They will be simultaneously conducting real-time online chat, identifying and demonstrating links and Web pages, identifying locations for specific bits of information and instructing the user how to conduct a more in-depth search.

While much of this sounds like what librarians are currently doing at a reference desk, it will be in an online atmosphere without the feedback clues to communication we know how to read, such as tone of voice or facial clues. While technology is developing low-cost cameras that allow us to see the patron, the tremendous increase in information sources will make the reference interview an even more complex process. The librarian will need a good understanding of information seeking and gathering behavior and information usage by individuals in order to determine how best to guide them through the plethora of information available.

The ability to work in groups will continue to be a necessary qualification. The composition of the groups is changing from the "reference team" composed entirely of reference librarians to cross-functional teams, which include staff who don't "speak" the language of reference. So a clear understanding of what we want to provide our users, and the ability of the librarian to explain it both orally and in writing, will be critical to the functioning of the team.

As libraries compete more with other information providers, we need librarians who can market the advantages of library services and who understand the economics of information provision. The many options for providing information and services need to be critically evaluated to ensure that we are getting the best return on our investment of human and fiscal resources. This requires librarians with analytical and critical thinking skills.

As they say, the more things change, the more things remain the same. As things change, we will continue to need librarians who can accurately assess current needs and connect that to a vision of how future programs, technology and services can effectively respond to changing user needs.

27

It Takes a
Cyber Librarian

Janet Foster

Despite the paradigm shift to electronic resources, traditional attributes that have been crucial for librarians in the past will continue to be just as relevant in the future. Interpersonal and communication skills will be integral characteristics for those in the public library sector. These skills are transcendent and universally acknowledged in any field of endeavor but especially for people considering a career in public librarianship.

Consider the plight of reference librarians who stand on the "front lines" at service desks on a daily basis. Patrons come to the library speaking a multitude of different languages. They may be seeking information about health, taxes and jobs or asking about reading programs for children. Quite often the information desk resembles a triage unit, or a control tower, with librarians acting as air traffic controllers. If you're not a people-oriented person, then perhaps public librarianship is not the best career move for you. But if you enjoy a fast-paced, interactive environment that is always changing, consider launching your career in the next generation as a public librarian.

While having people skills remains vital, being flexible is of inordinate importance. If you've worked in or used a public library in recent memory you've undoubtedly noticed a departure from the quiet, hushed tones of the past. Copiers, printers, computers and other peripheral devices create a cacophonous throng and odds are that there will be no single point in time when all the mechanical and electrical devices will be working simultaneously.

If you're a person who likes a set schedule and enjoys knowing what the day will be like ahead of time, public librarianship is probably not the avenue you want to pursue.

Flexibility and adaptability means being able to roll with the cyber punches—both good and bad. That new software program that promises to make your library life easier is also going to mean hours and hours of training—for staff, patrons and remote users. And when lightning strikes, literally or figuratively, and the power goes down, be ready to boot up all your computers and retrieve documents for cyber patrons.

Flexibility also means being ready for the patron who inserted a Mac-formatted disk into a PC and doesn't know why a document is corrupted. It means knowing how to convert a Word Perfect document into Microsoft or vice versa and using creative strategies to download documents from the Internet. That stubborn page that is trapped in a frame or the e-mail message that needs to be copied and pasted into a Word program or even printed using a screen dump are just some of the cyber obstacles that public librarians need to handle on a routine basis.

Public librarians can also expect to be heaped with gratitude by the senior patron who has just viewed a newborn grandchild via the Internet, or the person who found a job or another who learned a new language. Again, it's the people who matter most while the technology plays a secondary role. Hiring the most proficient, computer-savvy technician is not in the best interest of the public library if the person cannot demonstrate interpersonal skills.

Being a team player is essential. No librarian is an island. We are truly all connected in this brave new cyber world where your card catalog is likely now online and your patron records and material selection databases are interwoven into a fine, virtual fabric. Librarians at busy public libraries can expect interactions with each and every department. Some days it even seems as if there are interactions with staff members in Technical, Services, Administration, and Publicity, in addition to remote patrons and colleagues from other libraries.

The challenge then is to forward, process, upload or interpret the information to the appropriate team that handles the situation and knowing when to resolve a problem yourself. Certainly, we cannot all be experts in genealogy but we can get a patron started on researching in our local history rooms or via the Web or connecting with a local historical society.

And we can call on team members to help with everything from information searches to technical troubleshooting. Sometimes being the person who asks for help is more difficult than being the one providing assistance. Librarians should know their limitations and respect their intuition about asking for and receiving professional help from colleagues, staff members and sometimes even other patrons.

In the future, print materials and electronic data should be able to co-exist harmoniously in public library settings with the assistance of well-trained, flexible staff members who possess excellent communication and people skills. Despite the plethora of computer-related information, inter-action with patrons is still of pivotal importance for public librarians or librarians in any sector for that matter. Artificial intelligence is only plausible with human beings at the helm, creating, navigating and retrieving information in a variety of formats. Envision a future where instead of park benches, cyber patrons gather in virtual town halls to share ideas and convey opinions via their local public library. The possibilities seem limitless.

Cyberspace has lifted temporal constraints from many traditional librarian roles. Like the Olympic metaphor, "Citius, altius, fortius," [a Latin phrase meaning "swifter, higher, stronger"], librarians strive to deliver the best information in the least amount of time using their skills as leaders in the information delivery world. Librarians are accomplishing these goals in the face of daunting challenges, as they have in the past and will in the future. The Danbury Public Library's slogan, "From Text to Technology," epitomizes the role of the librarian in the 21st century. Whatever the format, the quest for knowledge and the desire of public librarians to assist patrons in "discovering the possibilities of their imaginations" (per the Danbury Public Library Mission Statement) remains a worthy and viable vision.[1]

NOTE

1. Useful URLs related to this subject include the American Library Association at *http://www.ala.org,* the American Library Association Bill of Rights at *http://www.ala.org/work/freedom/lbr.html,* Access to Electronic Information: An Interpretation of the Library Bill of Rights at *http://www.ala.org/alaorg/oif/electacc.html,* the Public Library Association at *http://www.pla.org* and the Danbury Public Library Mission Statement at *http://danburylibrary.org.*

28

The Academic Library—Not a Lair for Fiery Dragons

Barbara Burd

The librarians of today, and it will be true still more of the librarians
of tomorrow, are not fiery dragons interposed between the people
and the books.

They are the useful public servants, who manage libraries in the
interest of the public. . . . Many still think that a great reader, or a
writer of books, will make an excellent librarian. This is pure fal-
lacy.

—Sir William Osler, 1917

The library of today is a dynamic and challenging environment that offers
many opportunities to new librarians. We face the daily challenges of
bringing exemplary service and resources to a diverse community that
can exist anywhere in the world. The library without walls has become a
reality. While the delivery of services and resources has changed formats,
the basic values of our profession remain constant and it is in developing
these values that we find growth and success for our institutions and
ourselves. Michael Gorman (2000) states that the following values govern
our interactions within our communities: ". . . stewardship, service, intellectual freedom, rationalism, literacy and learning, equity of access to recorded knowledge and information, privacy, [and] democracy."[1]

Although these values are intrinsic to our profession, I would also suggest that new librarians focus on personal values to enhance their role as professionals. While many schools are forsaking the term library science in favor of information studies and many in our profession are adopting the title information specialist, today's librarians are much more than information specialists. We are more than providers of information or even specialists in information retrieval. We are communicators of knowledge, possessing the skills and abilities to share with others the tools to access, evaluate, analyze, and synthesize information into a knowledge base that is critical to the needs of the seeker. As such, we are even more than educators, possessing the resources to meet both the affective and cognitive needs of our patrons. As a new librarian, develop your personal values of integrity and respect for the individual. Traditionally librarians are thought to be idealistic and altruistic. While these values are often debunked in our society, they are the very values that set us apart—that can hold the most influence in our ability to shape the society in which we exist.

Today's academic librarian should develop an awareness of the culture of her library and the culture in which the library exists. To participate in the intellectual discourse so vital to the university community, the librarian should be involved in scholarly research. Guedon (1998) states, "Because libraries are too often regarded as a mere service and not as an essential part of research institutions, librarians tend to remain segregated from the research community in a fundamental way. There lies the main obstacle preventing libraries from playing an important role in redefining the political economy of knowledge." We, who have unlimited information at our fingertips, must also accept the responsibility for turning that information into knowledge that enhances our professional status.[2]

The future of the academic library lies in the ability of its librarians to collaborate with faculty. To do so, the librarian needs to be considered as an equal with faculty. As accreditation processes move toward integration of information literacy into the curriculum, the librarian is poised in a unique position. We possess the skills and abilities to become vital participants in the process, but we often lack the credibility to achieve collegial relationships. Librarians must assert themselves on their campus and be willing to be judged by the same standard as the rest of the faculty. Sharing the common values of scholarship and research provides a foundation for the relationships that can benefit both faculty and students. As new librarians it is imperative to participate in the intellectual communication that permeates the campus.

These are exciting times for libraries and librarians. Our borders are expanding in ways that have never before been possible. We have a choice.

We can cede our profession to those who would choose to remain simple "technology" or "information" experts or we can take this opportunity to develop our profession into something very special and unique. We have a strong tradition and a vital history founded on the core value of service. To maintain this tradition in an academic community competing in an information society, we must develop the values of intellectual discourse and scholarship to participate fully in the collegial undertakings of the university. As a new librarian, you have the opportunity, even the responsibility, to accept this challenge.

NOTES

1. Michael Gorman, *Our enduring values: Librarianship in the 21st century* (Chicago: American Library Association, 2000).

2. J. Guedon, "The virtual library: an oxymoron?" In *Medical Library Association: 1998 Joseph Leiter Lecture*. Retrieved from http://www.mlanet.org/publications/bmla/leiter98.html.

29

The Academic Librarian of the Future
The View from California Lutheran University

Susan Herzog

FROM ACADEMIC LIBRARIAN TO INFORMATION SPECIALIST

In 1994 the vision of Dr. Ken Pflueger, associate provost at California Lutheran University (CLU), became reality. Pflueger merged six departments, all related to various information services and technology, into one department called Information Systems and Services (ISS). The six sections which existed prior to 1994 were the Library, Media Services, Telecommunications, Academic Computing, Administrative Computing, and the Center for Instructional Multimedia. From 1994 to 1996, the new ISS consisted of an associate provost overseeing two sections: User Services and Technical Services.

Due to a blurring of the distinction between User and Technical Services, a second reorganization of ISS was undertaken in 1996 to form work groups around tasks. By 1997 Pflueger's vision of librarians as Information Specialists had come to fruition, following the creation of a

Reference and Instruction team. The Reference and Instruction team consisted of three librarians under a manager who shared the duties of the other Information Specialists.

Is Information Specialist Just a Fancy Name for a Librarian?

Prior to the formation of ISS, CLU, like other academic institutions, had Reference Librarians, a Collection Development Librarian and a Cataloger. By 1997 those positions no longer existed. Who filled the new positions and what qualifications were required? The CLU vision was an information professional, able to work with any and all information needs. The Information Specialists were all required to have ALA-accredited MLS degrees; in addition, experience and/or training in the following areas was also required:

- Reference
- Collection development
- Bibliographic instruction
- Computer software
- Internet applications

Information Specialists taught software and Internet applications to faculty, staff and students on campus. The primary focus was on Microsoft Office applications, e-mail, FTP, Internet searching and online calendar tools. If an Information Specialist needed additional training in order to teach computer software, there was a generous professional development fund available.

Web Pages

In 1998 Web page development became an integral part of the Information Specialists' duties; again, training was provided to augment existing skills. A generous grant from the Charles E. Culpeper Foundation brought salary for a fifth Information Specialist and a challenging mission: initiating a faculty-development program called Teaching, Technology, and Teamwork (TTT). Using a collaborative team approach, courses were redesigned to integrate technology into the curriculum. Each Culpeper project team included a faculty member (the subject matter expert), an Information Specialist (the researcher) and a student assistant who implemented the technology elements of the project.

Information Literacy and Management Responsibilities

As information literacy became a central concern of the Reference and Instruction team, we held an all-day retreat off-campus, designed a mission statement, and assessed our priorities. Following this retreat, we asserted that we wanted to spend more time on bibliographic instruction and information literacy and less time on computer training. In addition, we expressed interest in "flattening" our management model and taking on a team management initiative. This request led to a reorganization of the Reference and Instruction team during the summer of 2000; additionally, a subscription to an e-learning company was implemented and a Computer Training Coordinator was hired. The Information Specialists took on management responsibilities, each coordinating a library function:

1. Reference and undergraduate information literacy
2. Collection development (print, electronic databases and periodicals)
3. Library Webmaster and library systems
4. Access services (circulation and interlibrary loan) and graduate information literacy

The past year has been a challenge! Adding management responsibilities to our already full plates was, at times, a hardship; however, feedback from faculty indicates that the library hasn't been as effective in years.

Hiring New Information Specialists

Is the Information Specialist/Manager position more difficult than a more traditional academic library position? I believe that it is and I also believe that it's more fulfilling. For librarians aspiring to management positions in any setting, it is an excellent training ground. For those like myself, attracted by academic reference work with an emphasis on instruction, this is my dream job.

Recently, after three and four years respectively, two Information Specialists moved on and we recently hired two replacements. When résumés are received, the first sorting removes candidates without the basic ALA-accredited MLS. Once unqualified candidates are removed, the packet of résumés is routed to each Information Specialist, along with a résumé chart. The chart categories are:

- Reference experience
- Instruction experience

- Collection development experience
- Computer skills
- Web page development skills
- Professional library experience (especially in an academic setting)
- Other

The team reviews all the qualified candidates, making notes on our chart; you may be wondering about the "Other" category. We use it for specific talents like fluency in a foreign language, management experience or subject expertise.

After filling in our charts, we each make a list of ten front-runners and meet to develop a merged list, acceptable to all of us. Each of the ten candidates is called by the Information Specialist coordinating the current search to set up appointments for phone interviews. The responsibility of coordinating the search is rotated so that everyone gains this valuable experience.

Phone interviews are conducted via conference call or speaker-phone with at least two Information Specialists interviewing each candidate. We have a standard list of questions and each of us records our impressions. The next step is a meeting with all the Information Specialists where we whittle down our list to three to five top candidates for on-campus interviews.

The on-campus interview is an all-day affair. The candidate arrives at 9:00 A.M. for a tour of the campus, followed by an informal meeting with the paraprofessional staff. Next, the candidate is given half an hour to prepare for an instruction session in our electronic classroom. The instruction session varies from year to year; usually we ask the candidate to demonstrate teaching a new database and we provide them with one to two weeks' preparation time and IP-validated access to the database. We invite the entire ISS staff to be the students for the candidate's instruction session. Each staff member fills out an evaluation form following the session.

The Library Director, the Information Specialists, and one or two faculty members take the candidate out to lunch followed by a formal interview with prepared questions. Following the interview, the candidate meets with the Library Director. At every stage of the interview, candidates are invited to ask any questions they may have. Following the interviews, the Information Specialist in charge of the search gathers all the paperwork, delegates Endnotes to be checked and solicits recommendations at a formal meeting.

One last word on our model: it can be challenging to find a person who meets most of our requirements and, if a candidate is particularly strong in a crucial area, we are always prepared to be flexible. Our Library Director is exceptionally generous with time and money for professional development in order to build the requisite skills.

30

The FAKTs of Life

Being a Small-College Librarian

Molly Flaspohler

So, you want to be a 21st-century academic librarian at a small college? That's great! We need you. If you are lively and bright, I couldn't be more pleased. But before we get too excited, take it from someone whose friends still marvel that this former sorority president chose libraries; the profession requires different skills and energies than those you may expect if you still hear the voice of Charlie Brown's invisible teacher, no matter how faintly, every time you think "librarian." So, the first piece of advice is to get over the stereotyping. Don't let yourself get caught up in that age-old discussion. Ignore it. While a certain amount of self-deprecating humor about your profession will assuredly come in handy when faced with twenty-five less-than-interested college freshmen and a sixty-minute one-shot library session, freeing yourself from the idea that what you do is somehow "uncool" is the first step to becoming a great success. Academic librarians of the future know that what they teach is critically important and that the information they have to share can make a real difference to students who are anxious, overwhelmed, and Internet-dependent.

After ten years of doing this job, there are four traits that I have found especially valuable for librarians hoping to serve smaller academic institutions. Though it may be a tired convention, I've come up with my own little acronym. Librarians in the 21st century need to get the "FAKTs." That is to say, they need to be Flexible, Articulate, Kind, and Tenacious. I should also add that these four traits are in addition to the assumption that savvy librarians will at a minimum be appropriately educated, possess basic communication skills, and know more than a little something about computer equipment and electronic resources.

To say that academic librarians at smaller institutions need to be flexible is an enormous understatement. In any single day you may have to make a presentation to a faculty committee, teach a class of less-than-enthusiastic students, diplomatically explain to a faculty member why an assignment requiring all thirty-five of his or her students to find book reviews on the same book may not work very well, un-jam any number of printing devices, and find a complete list of diseases fish can get. Trust me, days like this exist, I've had them. Future librarians must possess an ability to deal with rapid, constant change. Prepare yourself for the fact that over time your students will change, your job responsibilities will change and the resources you utilize to do your job will change . . . a LOT. If you find honing your flexibility skills exciting and the challenge of adapting to change invigorating, librarianship will be a great profession for you.

Academic librarians are called on at many levels to explain what it is we do and why we do it. It is therefore imperative that future members of the profession be able to articulate a clear understanding of complex issues relating to a wide array of subjects like information literacy and assessment, advancing information technologies, copyright and plagiarism, and so forth. But, beyond an ability to write and speak clearly within the profession, librarians must also possess the facility to recognize when we are not using the appropriate language with our audiences. Future academic librarians must connect with an increasingly diverse population of 21st-century students. These same librarians must also collaborate regularly with faculty who are traditionally more homogeneous in terms of learning and teaching styles. Capable academic librarians will need to recognize a widening disparity between the groups of patrons we serve and articulate creative new ways for thinking about and using the library effectively.

Simplistic as it sounds, I believe one of the most valuable traits a successful academic librarian can demonstrate is kindness. Having grown up in the Midwest, I recognize that the risk for sounding naively "Minnesota-nice," as we phrase it here, is great. Yet, after working with undergraduates for so long, my belief in the importance of this attribute continues to grow. Students have become many things over the last ten years. They are consumer oriented, computer literate and hip-hop cultured; they are grown-up and media savvy in ways we wouldn't think possible. Yet, most students remain quite fearful about asking for help in the library. They cast furtive glances at the Reference desk ("If I don't make eye contact with the librarian, she won't know I'm having trouble."). Or, if they are brave enough to approach us, they say, "I know this is a stupid question, but . . . ." At the very minimum, we can reduce these students' fear of librarians and the library. Academic librarians of the 21st century have to *want* to work with students of all ages and from a variety of backgrounds. Skilled librarians need to be friendly and extremely approachable. They should be willing to take on the role of mentor, and in some cases, friend. If you are considering academic librarianship, take a real interest in your students' educational studies and their goals. Get involved with their projects. Listen to their concerns. Be a nice person. It's extremely important to the patrons you serve.

Finally, future academic librarians need to be tenacious. This trait will be especially useful after explaining to faculty for the 642nd time why scavenger hunts are not a good idea only to learn later that the confused freshman standing in front of you at your next Reference shift has been expressly told by his or her professor not to bother librarians with exactly this type of "fun" library activity. Face it, there are a lot of faculty who simply don't understand libraries. Surprisingly, some of them won't *want* to understand us. Academics at small institutions are often overextended, overwhelmed, and they already have a disciplinary specialty, thank you very much. Libraries and information literacy will probably never be their top priority. Which is why librarians have to be tenacious, persistent, and yes, even sneaky. If a faculty member seems particularly library challenged, find a way to tactfully communicate why an assignment isn't working well. If they don't get it the first time, go back and offer specific alternatives; gently point out the distress their students are having. Use subterfuge if you have to (ask the professor to help you work with students on the assignment in the library, see if together you can identify where the assignment needs to be refined). If the problem continues, remember that faculty members do not wake up in the morning thinking of ways to intentionally drive librarians insane. Doggedly go back again. Keep the lines of communication open. Remember the students you serve and be tenacious.

31

Why a Good "Sh-h-h" Doesn't Cut It Anymore

Personality Characteristics of the 21st-Century Librarian

Maria C. Bagshaw

When I decided to get my MLS in 1994, the running jokes with my husband and his family were:

"When are you going to graduate with your 'official librarian's bun'?"and "Have you had the class on effective 'shushing'?"

Needless to say, these stereotypes were at best amusing and at worst aggravating. However, I found out throughout my schooling that, depending on individual experience, most people regarded librarians as quiet, unattractive and often downright cantankerous. In fact, many people I knew couldn't believe that I was going to be a librarian: I didn't look, behave or sound like what the perception of a librarian was. I became determined to become the opposite of the stereotype: helpful, fun and sympathetic.

In the 1980s, the popular game show *Family Feud* surveyed 100 people for the top typical characteristics of librarians. The top three responses were:

1. Quiet
2. Mean/stern
3. Single/unmarried

There are several works in the field of librarianship that discuss the portrayal of librarians in the media and movies, many of which have no doubt contributed to these perceptions. Even in my experience, many students have described me as a "nice" or "very helpful" librarian, unlike "the one I grew up with at my hometown school/public library." With these perceptions still entrenched in people's psyches, whether warranted or not, there is a need to actively change the stereotypes of librarians from negative to positive.[1]

As the market for librarians is shrinking in this downsized economy and competition is becoming fiercer, successful librarians will need to possess most, if not all, of the characteristics cited below. The concept of the library itself is changing from one of a depository of static, archival information to a dynamic housing of many types of media and an exploding overabundance of information from which to choose. With the end user often skipping the information mediary (that's us, the librarians), we need to morph from keepers of knowledge to the facilitators of knowledge management. No more quiet, meek or stern personalities; today's librarians need to possess outgoing, friendly, positive characteristics for survival in a world where many people see libraries and librarians as obsolete.

The ten characteristics below offer a good guideline for success in the 21st-century library:

1. Openness: ability to be nonjudgmental and open-minded regardless of the subject matter and personal beliefs;
2. Friendliness: ability to smile and use other body language to let the patron know that you sincerely want to help and care about the success and quest for knowledge that he or she seeks;
3. Persistence: ability to see the question/problem through "to the end"—either with a cited answer or with a referral to someone who can help the patron. This includes the ability to keep good records, so that if that question recurs or you discover the answer you can answer the question or contact the original patron with additional information.
4. Flexibility: ability to handle multiple questions/problems at once while maintaining friendliness and professionalism; also, the ability to try many different, even unconventional, avenues, in order to find the answer.
5. Teaching ability: taking a question/problem down to its "lowest common denominator"; for example, when teaching new skills or computer programs, begin at the very beginning, assume nothing, and let the patron set the pace of learning.

6. Patience: ability to redirect, rethink questions and go over the same concept several times without frustration or making the patron feel uncomfortable. REALLY make sure that the patron is "getting it."

7. Communication: ability to do the reference interview in a nonthreatening way, explaining as you question WHY you are asking so many questions if the patron seems uncomfortable. Make sure the patron does not feel like this is the Inquisition (especially if it is a sensitive topic).

8. Personal attention: ability to make each individual feel that you are working exclusively on his or her problem, and applying persistence to see the question/problem through to its natural conclusion. You may need to work on several problems at once, but avoid answering the phone or being interrupted by other patrons during the reference interview if possible.

9. Subject knowledge: ability to be a generalist, i.e., becoming familiar with as many subject areas as you can, including computer/technology troubleshooting. Unless you are planning on working solely in one subject area, "knowledge is power!"

And most important . . .

10. Love of the game: you need to love being a librarian and enjoy helping people reach their goals. Having the foresight to determine the needs of both your library and your patrons will benefit how your library and librarians in general are viewed.

In conclusion, today's libraries are dynamic, busy and sometimes noisy places. They are no longer the dark, dusty archives of the past. They can be very exciting places for adults and children alike, constantly changing due to the variety of information and media available and the new formats constantly being invented. By applying the above characteristics, librarians will further enhance their reputations to reflect the knowledgeable, exciting and service-oriented individuals that they are.

"Sh-h-h" doesn't cut it anymore; librarians need to *shout* their knowledge and expertise from the rooftops and make themselves indispensable to their patrons.

NOTE

1. C.A. Kirkendall, "Of Princess Di, Richard Dawson and the Book Review Digest (how bibliographic instruction librarians are changing stereotypes for libraries)," *Research Strategies* 4 (1986): 40–42.

32

The Future
of Librarianship

Felix T. Chu

The Summer 2001 issue of *Journal of Education for Library and Information Science* included many papers about the Kellogg-ALISE Information Professions and Education Reform Project (KALIPER). This project was a study about the state of library and information science curricula. Sutton remarked that a user-centered perspective has infused the curricula at some schools, thus marking a Copernican shift from studying the content of libraries to learning about those who consume the content.[1] But what of the librarians who occupy the space in between the content and the users? Who can best fit the role of the intermediary? That space in-between marks the future of librarianship.

In reading about librarianship, experiencing the environment in which we work, and reflecting on current trends in practice and research, it is apparent that many of us are not shifting paradigms to meet the changes around us at an appropriate rate. As libraries and library education expanded during the middle part of the 20th century, we embraced a positivistic outlook that emphasized absolutes. If only we can find the right methodology for a research study, a right trend in collection development, or arrive at the right question, we can then unequivocally supply the right answer. The manifestations of this positivism are all around us. We have the "best" reference sources, reviews indicating the "appropriate" books for a small college library, and standards that indicate the desired wording of reference encounters.

In the past few decades, other disciplines have been moving away from positivism. Articles suggesting alternatives have started appearing. Many have come to the conclusion that the value of information is socially defined.[2] The requirements for institutional accreditations all have guidelines that specify assessments and self-studies. One of the major undertakings is crafting a distinct mission statement for each institution and units within that institution. Assessment then becomes a check on how well one adheres to that mission. However, the institutional mission is not a shared statement. It is a statement that reflects local realities. Assessment thus is local in nature. Within this environment, there is no adherence to an absolute value that one strives for as in positivism.

In 1934, José Ortega y Gasset talked about the mission of the librarian in his address to the International Congress of Bibliographers and Librarians in Paris.[3] He concluded by saying that within this social environment, the librarian of the future must function as a filter between the reader and the torrent of books. If one thinks of the book as a symbol for all information and information sources available to a library patron, then our mission becomes that of acting as an intermediary between the patron and the library collection, including those available online in different formats. If one accepts this argument, then our mission has not changed. The future librarian will try to achieve what we are trying to do.

It is just that technology has changed. So our goals and tools have changed. In revisiting Ortega's ideas in his article in 1982, Lester Asheim went further with the metaphor of the filter to talk about a ventilation system.[4] In that case, the task becomes not only pushing out the bad air and allowing in fresh air but also regulating the amount of exchange to maintain a proper balance. He went on to say that in regard to communications, the intent is not a quantitative measure that allows in sounds that exceed a certain decibel. "Noise" that is to be kept out is that which does not have the appropriate content. This of course leads to the understanding that noise for one patron is not necessarily noise for another patron. Similarly, the best reference source for one patron may not be the best source for another patron even though they have posed similar questions.

To refine the idea of a filter, one must keep in mind that the filter cannot be a static tool and what the filter allows in and keeps out at a given instance does not really disappear. It is a matter of what is to be brought into the foreground and what is to be kept in the background. In an earlier article, I talked about frames to be used in a reference encounter.[5] The frames, originally discussed by Lee Bolman and Terrence Deal in the management of educational institutions, are structural, human resource, political, and symbolic. They refer respectively to the organization's fit with environment and technology, workings with people, conflict resolution through political knowledge and skills, and the use of rites and metaphors. Each frame functions as a lens that sharpens certain features while dimming other attributes.

Even though the basic mission has not changed for librarians, what has changed and will keep changing is the environment that determines the social construction of what we call information. We catalog and index not only books and journal articles but also online resources to increase access. But the paradox is that the access points are frozen at the time of cataloging according to the understanding of the cataloger even though users create new jargon and realign discipline cores in that changing environment.[6] With the increasing pace of environmental change, this paradox is no longer trivial. So a librarian must be sensitive to that paradox and be able to help in bridging that gap between the creation of access points and time of need.

A librarian would function as a dynamic filter for Ortega y Gasset. That filter then also takes on the role of balancing. In using the idea of frames, a multidimensional component is introduced where a librarian must deal with a dynamic window with changeable lenses that would allow multiple views of information in creating multiple realities. Thus a librarian must embrace continuous learning not only of technology but also new frames of reference and paradigms. More importantly, the meaning that one derives is from contextualizing one's library and one's work within the environment. This is my view of one aspect of the future.

NOTES

1. Stuart A. Sutton, "Trends, Trend Projections, and Crystal Ball Gazing," *Journal of Education for Library and Information Science* 42 (Summer 2001): 241–47.

2. See, for example, *The Social Life of Information* by John Seely Brown and Paul Duguid (Boston: Harvard Business School Press, 2000).

3. José Ortega y Gasset, "The mission of the librarian," trans. James Lewis and Ray Carpenter, *The Antioch Review* 21 (Summer 1961): 133–54.

4. Lester Asheim, "Ortega revisited," *Library Quarterly* 52 (July 1982): 215–26.

5. Felix T. Chu, "Framing reference encounters," *RQ* 36 (Fall 1996): 93–101.

6. Felix T. Chu, "The freezing of dynamic knowledge," *Technicalities* 16 (January 1966): 1, 7–9. Since new subject headings are always trailing development, subject access using standard library tools will reflect an understanding of the discipline at the time of cataloging or indexing.

33

Arrogance

For Obvious Reasons

Shelley Ross

A healthy dose of the right kind of arrogance is essential for novice and experienced librarians. We should evidence pride in our worthy profession. The librarianship I'm proud of is characterized by devotion to uniformity, ease of access, and reluctance to forbid. When it turned out that the Mars Climate Orbiter fell victim to conflicting systems of measurement, did anyone else reflect on our almost universal devotion to AACR2, LCSH and MARC? At a time when most everybody and their grandmother can jump headfirst onto the Internet and find all sorts of information, which profession started talking about cataloging and providing field-based identity information long before meta tags became trendy? Which profession is concerned with bridging the growing divide between digital haves and have-nots? We librarians know we're needed more than ever. So where does arrogance come in? If we can be arrogant about our expertise, and if our arrogance has a foundation in extreme competence, then we can expect people to ask for and take to heart our learned advice.

Let's talk about the sort of arrogance I'd like us to cultivate. Consider how many of the "big men" on a campus near you could reasonably be described as arrogant. If you are universally acknowledged as the best neurobiologist on campus you might just as well accept your rank with a certain kind of arrogance. When you speak to issues in neurobiology your opinion carries weight because you are very fit to comment. Supplicants know that it makes more sense to ask your opinion than to try to formulate their own. And there's work involved: the price of arrogance is the constant struggle to stay abreast of your area of expertise. When people ask your opinion you drop everything to come up with an answer that seems casual in its effort but which is, in fact, based on hard and efficient work. When you dispense your pearls of wisdom you do so in such a manner as to make it clear that you can provide as much proof as anyone can handle, but really, they should accept the fruits of your deep thinking and leave the process to the professionals who truly understand the arguments. It may take twenty minutes to perfect the tone and wording of a two-paragraph e-mail. What's important is that your arrogance—your deeply held sense that you have every right to the last word on the topic—is deserved. You've done the homework and you don't rest on your laurels.

That other kind of arrogance, the undeserved kind, the kind of arrogance that assumes too much on title and position, will only get you into trouble. If you're going to take up the burden of a high sense of worth you'd better pick a concentrated area and be prepared to do a lot of reading and practicing. You don't speak to every single issue that comes up, you wait for the ones that fall into your area of expertise.

It's easy for librarians to respect arrogance in others. We are intimately aware of the depth and breadth of literature in any field our patrons can imagine. We know that "I looked but there's nothing on my topic" is almost universally untrue. But when was the last time you heard a librarian described as arrogant? You versus Einstein: the topic is relativity—and the winner is Einstein. You versus Einstein: the topic is Boolean logic for undergrads—and the winner is, that's right, you. We are disciples in a profession which has serious content. I know that, you know that, even the freshest and most inexperienced of recent library school graduates are soon to discover it. Why do we have such trouble claiming our expertise?

Name another profession that worries as much as we do about using language and strategies that constantly minimize the complexity of the information systems we employ. When we teach, do reference work, create bibliographic guides and tools, and describe activities to those outside our profession, we go to great lengths to eliminate jargon, simplify concepts, and treat library research as a simple and easy thing. We do these things for good reasons and with the best of intentions. But is it any surprise that administrators think they know everything we do, maybe more, about running libraries? Why are we offended when our non-library faculty offer helpful suggestions about our library practice? It seems to me that a tasteful amount of arrogance goes a long way to reducing the expectation that we desperately need guidance and leadership while at the same time giving our users the comfort of knowing that library matters are in competent library hands.

Standard practice is to treat every well-meant suggestion that we should consider resource sharing with another library with grave seriousness, at least until we're safely in our office and able to laugh. Perhaps we should bristle at the suggestion that libraries have not always been at the forefront when it comes to sharing our catalogs, employing appropriate technology, and leading the way in fair access to information.

Here's a short course in Arrogance 101 for Librarians:

Be excellent: Don't pretend to know stuff. If someone asks a question and you don't know the answer, tell them you'll get back to them. And do so, as quickly as possible. If it turns out you were wrong about something, make sure you tell the patrons before they figure it out for themselves. When a new database comes online, make sure you read the FAQs or most likely HELP information, if nothing else. If you're helping some persons with something you aren't familiar with, let them know that, and explain that you'll figure it out together. Share a bit of your hierarchical knowledge with them ". . . databases should allow you to limit searches, let's see how this one does it." Get to know as much about your library as you are able. Read or at least scan the professional literature. Listen to staff but don't let your vision be limited by the tried and true.

Be prompt: When patrons make a request or suggestion make sure you respond immediately. I'm a science librarian in a cash-strapped institution. Most of my initial contact with faculty involves them asking for materials and me telling them I have no money to buy anything. They have every reason to consider me unhelpful. But I never make them wait for a response. And I always try to give simple and factual reasons. When possible I offer an alternative. Although I may be careful to use the rhetorical strategy of suggesting that they already know what I'm about to say, I go on to say it in some detail, and offer professional reasons—privacy, freedom of access to information, preservation, and so on, that the other person is unlikely to have considered. They need to be reminded, gently but frequently, that they don't know how to do your job. When they quit assuming that they do, you can lay off a little.

Be a promoter: Know about your discipline. If you weren't paying attention in library school, and I wasn't, bone up on at least the highlights of library history. Pay attention to the exceptional cooperation and compromise which are the hallmarks of our success. If some psychology professor thinks Medline is the greatest thing since sliced bread, make sure that you give credit to the librarians who came up with it every chance you get. If they think the citation indexes are indispensable, make sure that the librarian who came up with the idea—Eugene Garfield—gets credit. Don't say " the university" when you mean "the library," don't say "the budget" when you mean "my budget" or "the library budget for chemistry collections."

Use jargon: When faculty members complain about the difficulties of searching by subject in your catalog, in a sentence or two let them know about the long-standing, worldwide application of LCSH. If you're using e-mail make all the acronyms links to good explanatory sources, but use our professional language and jargon. Specialized language is the hallmark of a discipline and, while we must avoid using it when we wish to teach and encourage, it's a great tool when we need to remind others that they are tendering opinions in someone else's discipline. In a sentence or two make it clear that the simple question is a part of a much bigger and older issue, but then offer a graceful alternative—here are a variety of potential LCSH terms, I'll see to adding them to the record.

Be touchy: Take ownership of your expertise and don't let people trample all over you. If you wouldn't presume to tell them how to do their job, don't passively accept and even thank them for telling you how to do yours. Be gracious, but don't let an opportunity for gentle correction go by.

34

Developing Business and Management Skills for the 21st-Century Academic Librarian

John Riddle

The 21st-century academic librarian must be a manager. This may seem like an odd pronouncement to those who would say that librarians have always been managers: of collections, services, entire libraries. What I mean is that the 21st-century academic librarians must continue to adapt, and adapt better than they have, the tools and strategies of business and management to conduct their profession.[1]

My intention here is not to rehash the argument as to whether academic libraries should be envisioned as a kind of business, whether they should jettison a public service model that some would claim has caused the profession to lag behind the private sector in the effective development and marketing of information products and services.[2] One can avoid this debate yet still make the argument that many very successful business practices can be used by libraries to more efficiently conduct their work. Whatever the broader philosophical and social differences that exist between the public and private sectors, one thing is clear: businesses know how to manage, and much can be learned from business for the improved efficiency of library operations. The successful 21st-century librarian will know this and seek out proven management strategies and tools.

I said above that libraries must "continue to adapt" these practices, as many of the tools and methods of business have already been incorporated into the library structure. For instance, the increasing efficiency of interlibrary loan mirrors the just-in-time (JIT) concept of inventory management. Likewise, analyses of finance tools such as zero-based budgeting and PPBS (planning, programming, budgeting system) have found their ways into many books and articles on library management.[3]

Can academic libraries operate more efficiently? Of course they can. They must, given the almost certain future of shrinking staffs and budgets coupled with greater calls for positive outcome assessments. ("Prove you can do more with the less we're going to give you," the college administrator says between the lines.) Can librarians find techniques and tools in the business sector to improve efficiency while at the same time staying true to their public service mission? A resounding yes.

Successful management tools and strategies need to be used not only by library directors, but also by front-line librarians who can find and use many successful business practices to enhance their daily work. One example is the human resource technique of behavior-based candidate selection that can be adapted by 21st-century librarians serving on search committees.

Many academic librarians would be hard pressed to think of a professional activity more time consuming, more challenging, more laden with responsibility than serving on a search committee. A successful 21st-century librarian can take a leadership role on these committees by urging his or her colleagues to use candidate selection techniques proven to more closely match the needs of the position with the professional behaviors of the candidate.

The behavioral-based candidate selection process, derived from the fields of industrial psychology and organizational development, sees the search committee as the locus for the candidate to present examples of those behaviors that most closely match the needs of the position in question, what is called behavioral-based interviewing. And behavioral-based interviewing is just one part of this sophisticated selection process. At the beginning of its work, before interviewing has begun, the search committee should carefully examine the requirements of the position, not just for the skill levels needed, but also to analyze the various behavioral dimensions associated with it.

For instance, the job in question may require extensive evening or weekend hours. Instead of asking the candidate how he or she feels about working evenings or weekends (to which, of course, any sensible candidate who wants to keep even a foot in the door will answer "no problem"), the behavior focus search committee will first determine which particular behaviors are needed for successful performance during weekend or evening hours. It may be that the search committee is really looking for someone who can make independent decisions in the absence of an immediate supervisor, can handle multiple supervisory tasks for a range of professionals, para-professionals, and staff, and can deal successfully with the kinds of patrons who may frequent this particular library during these hours. These are the "behaviors" the search committee is really after, in addition to simply finding out whether the candidate can or cannot work the particular hours, or whether he or she has worked such hours in the past.

Behavioral-related interviewing would ask the candidate to relate a past experience in which she or he engaged in this kind of behavior, e.g., "Tell me of a time when you had to make a difficult decision on your own," "Tell me of a time when you had to work with a difficult (client or patron)," and so forth. The candidate would be prompted to ensure that he or she in fact related an example of actual past experience, avoiding hypothetical or general statements. If the candidate began his or her answer with "Whenever I have a difficult patron . . ." or "I always deal with difficult patrons . . ." he or she would be asked to relate a particular experience, with a real patron or situation. As one author has put it, the candidate is urged to "tell a story."[4]

Both positive and negative examples of past behaviors would be elicited. The search committee would need to know not only about success stories, but how the candidate dealt with problematic situations as well. The full range of the candidates' professional behaviors in various situations are brought to light through behavioral-based interviewing.

Behavior-related interviewing is only one example of the kinds of advanced management tools the successful 21st-century academic librarian can bring to the library profession. In this sense, going back to the beginning of this essay, the librarian "manages" his or her professional work. He or she seeks out and brings to the work environment management tools and strategies that have been shown to work in private business. The successful 21st-century librarian will not shirk these management skills because they smack of private business. Instead, these librarians will emerge as leaders, not just in high-level positions as library directors and deans, but among front-line professional staffs who realize that successful management of day-to-day operations—for instance, search committees—is equally vital for the advancement of the library profession.

NOTES

1. The argument of this essay pertains primarily to libraries in higher education institutions as that is where the author has gained most of his experience. It would seem, however, that much of the logic expressed here can be applied to public and school libraries. Of course, corporate libraries will most likely already have acquired many of the more successful business practices, in many cases moving ahead of their public-sector counterparts. One reads, for instance, much more about the concept and practice of knowledge management in special library- and corporate library-oriented journals than in general- and higher education-focused publications.

2. Consider, for instance, the storm that erupted recently over the suggestion that library online catalogs should emulate Amazon.com, or the controversy over the for-profit dot-com company Questia, delivering a product and service directly in competition with, and some would say superior to, traditional libraries. Also, the "virtual university" concept embodied by the University of Phoenix has aggressively used many of the marketing and client niche strategies of the business world, again to the chagrin of many librarians.

3. See, for example, Stueart and Moran, *Library and Information Center Management*, 4th ed. (Englewood, CO: Libraries Unlimited, 1993).

4. Hagevik, S., "Behavioral Interviewing: write a story, tell a story," *Journal of Environmental Health* 62, no. 7 (March 2000): 61, 76.

35

The 21st-Century Librarian

David H. Stanley

The challenges that face the 21st-century librarian are outgrowths of those that began appearing at the close of the last century. What one sees now is a growth of them on a much grander scale and development at a must faster rate. With this being the case, librarians are being called on to be more and more responsible for what goes on in their libraries and being called on to deal with issues not foreseen in years past. The majority of the challenges are in the areas of technology and collection development; although there are other areas that need to be examined.

The librarian of today must keep more and more on the cutting edge of many areas of technology. Online databases, not to mention Internet sites themselves, are proliferating in greater numbers; and although they do make one's ability to do research more encompassing, they also create a learning curve that must be continuously reevaluated. If librarians are to assist patrons in making the most of these innovations, then the librarians themselves must keep one step or more ahead in their uses and knowledge of the data available. This knowledge should encompass not only the use of databases but also the knowledge necessary to expertly evaluate the findings. With the ability to gather vast quantities of information it is an added responsibility for the librarian to examine, evaluate, and produce a more manageable and cohesive collection of information for the patron.

As this growth of Internet usage and databases becomes available and as even the smallest of libraries become connected, the librarian must also hone his or her skills in determining what can financially be offered in the library. A great development in getting more out of the purchasing power of the library dollar has been the creation of library consortia. Purchased by a single institution, the price of some of the more popular databases can be fiscally prohibitive. By joining with other libraries it is possible to get costs down to some very affordable rates. For any but the most affluent libraries this is the best way to ensure that the patrons are being given access to the best research material available online. But while consortial participation can make great strides in stretching a library budget to better serve the users, it is still up to the librarians to determine which of the many consortia best suit their needs. It is now not uncommon for one library to belong to more than one consortium in order to get the best offers from more than one vendor.

While the knowledge of searching is important, so it is necessary to have some understanding of the operation of personal computers themselves. It is the lucky librarian who has not had technical problems while in the middle of a reference or research project. The understanding of how to troubleshoot and solve many of the commonly occurring problems can make the librarian's job much easier. This rudimentary need to grasp the workings of a PC are greatly magnified if the library technology is under the supervision of a systems librarian as opposed to a trained computer technology specialist. In this situation the librarian must possess knowledge in the areas of PC repair, hardware and software installation and maintenance, as well as an understanding of computer networking, LANs, and program writing.

Coupled with the above areas is the growing expectation of librarians having to monitor the use of the Internet. In public libraries this goes so far as being expected to "cybersit" young people to ensure that the Internet is not used for noneducational purposes. There are also now more instances where the issue of censorship is called into play. This subject runs the gamut from filters on public access computers to the continual questioning of what types of items are suitable for inclusion in a library's collection. The American Library Association has issued statements on censorship; and while it seems to be clear how these issues should be handled, it is becoming less cut and dried. More and more of the guidelines that have been taken for granted by the library professional are being questioned not only by the patrons but by groups who are not even familiar with a library's holdings. As written works continue to broach areas that were not available in the past, it is probable that in some locations the practice of questioning a librarian's right as well as a library's rights to make decisions in collection development will continue to prosper. These are areas where the librarian, the library director, and the governing boards must work together. The best way to deal with these types of situations is to determine the protocol to handle them before they arise. Having policy in place before it is needed is the most effective way to deal with them if, or when, they arise.

Along with technology, public relations is a growing necessity for libraries. With the cost of purchasing library materials growing at a level that greatly outpaces inflation, Friends of the Library groups, the writing of grant applications, and the solicitation of funding sources are areas in which more library professionals are becoming deeply involved. These along with the annual request for more funding from public library boards of trustees and academic library administrations have given librarians greater experience in the public relations aspects of library operations. An added bonus from this area of work is the increased awareness of the library in the community—something that can work in the library's best interests while reinforcing its value to the locale that it serves.

Finally, whether those in our profession are referred to as librarians, information specialists, or by other names, the use of more traditional research methods must continue to be encouraged. A large amount of library resources continues to be spent on the purchase of books and periodicals. These items can greatly add to the reference quality of the Internet. Although there are vast amounts of information available via the Internet, books, journals, and other library holdings will continue to play an important part in the continued existence of institutions that have been serving people for centuries. One needs to be aware that this will not satisfy all users, since along with housing information for the patrons' use, the library is now also looked on as a place for those not able or willing to connect to the Internet in their own homes to gain access to the information highway. Where once the library was used to satisfy the informational and intellectual needs of its patrons, it is now also looked at as a babysitter and somewhere to go to get free access to the latest technology. These new uses will always involve the librarians who oversee the use of these buildings.

With all that is happening in our field the librarians of the 21st century are lucky to be part of an exhilarating time of change and development.

As long as one is able to find information for patrons or to be of assistance in showing patrons how to do their own research, we will be paving the way for continual development in all areas of the information sciences. This is a time for change made in great strides, and the challenge should be taken as an opportunity for all librarians to look toward the future with much excitement and enthusiasm.

36

Academic Reference as a Second Career

Cheryl Gunselman

"A wise man will make more opportunities than he finds."
—Francis Bacon

This essay begins with an assumption: as a profession, part of our obligation to the 21st century is identifying potential future librarians, and effectively communicating useful information about librarianship to this population. This essay is intended as an exploration of issues and challenges associated with one particular path to the profession: a midlife career change to librarianship, and, more specifically, to academic reference.

What is the "talent pool" from which academic librarians emerge? There are "naturals" in librarianship as in any other profession—individuals who know from an early age that they will be librarians, and who move systematically through their academic work, securing their first professional positions in their twenties or early thirties. And then there are others, potential librarians who initially pursue other professions. Some of these individuals may suspect when they are young that they would make good librarians, and might even consciously consider pursuing a career in the profession, but ultimately choose other options that seem more attractive. And there are those who are intellectually and temperamentally suited for librarianship, but who have overlooked the profession when making their career decisions. If we wish to give serious consideration to the issue of recruiting the best possible librarians for the 21st century, mature individuals who have had experience and success in other endeavors should be targeted. To the extent that they are not, and if they do not discover and choose librarianship through their own personal investigations, their loss represents an opportunity cost for the future of the profession.

These "potential librarians" are problem solvers by nature, and are likely to be known by their friends and co-workers as "answer people." They may be found in almost any organization, and display a natural tenacity and skill when faced with an information problem. If their abilities and efforts are not rewarded or valued by their organizations, if this problem-solving activity is peripheral to their primary job responsibilities, or if they feel dissatisfied with their work for other reasons, these individuals constitute a pool of potential talent, and should be considered as attractive candidates for recruitment into librarianship.

Changing careers at midlife is serious business: it is a complicated undertaking, and may require a long period of deliberation and preparation. An individual may identify librarianship as a good personal and professional fit, but then encounter barriers to entry, such as geography, time, and money (both educational expenses and salary issues). These constraints may play a larger role in the decision-making process for an individual at midlife; leaving a job and relocating to attend an ALA-accredited program may involve uprooting a family, with the prospect of a second relocation upon completion of the degree. Personal risk-reward calculations become more complex, with the risk of a poor career choice seeming higher at midlife—even without taking into account the best interests of other family members. Financial considerations also play a role in the decision-making process, as the relatively low salaries for entry-level librarians are likely to entail a salary cut for an individual making a midlife career change; the perception of substantial "intangible" rewards is needed to compensate for the salary gap.

PUBLIC AWARENESS

Useful information about the profession of librarianship needs to be made more visible and more accessible. Our "talent pool" of natural problem-solvers might reasonably be expected to find essential information about the profession on their own, but would also benefit from recruitment literature produced by our professional associations. With respect to reference librarianship, topics might include: comparative information about reference work in public, academic, school and special libraries; academic preparation for reference librarianship; basic information about core competencies; and discussion about the profession from current practitioners. It certainly could be argued that these topics are covered in the professional literature. But it is important to recognize that these articles are generally directed toward an audience of current practitioners rather than members of the public, including prospective librarians.[1] In her article "Libraries in the New Millennium and Political Realities," Martha Gould addresses recruitment challenges among other issues. Noting a recent *Occupational Outlook Quarterly* forecast of 39,000 librarian position openings over the next decade, she considers the likelihood of a shortage of qualified professionals to fill them. She calls for an active response: "Creative recruitment, which is more than just scholarship programs, must be done at the local, state and national levels by our professional associations and state associations." She asserts that the leadership for this recruitment effort should be local, coming from state librarians.[2]

The "intangible" rewards of librarianship, as mentioned earlier, are also central to awareness about the profession. They may be found in the work itself, in the nature of libraries as institutions and working environments, and in our professional culture. In addition to objective statements about these professional rewards, stories about personal experiences are also helpful to individuals as they consider what it would be like to be an academic reference librarian. Particularly for those considering moving out of careers in business, the movement into a "helping" culture from a profit-motivated one may be very appealing.

ACADEMIC PREPARATION

With the ALA-accredited master's degree as the primary entry credential for academic librarianship in the United States, and a limited number of ALA-accredited institutions, geography is a potential obstacle for mature adults seeking career-change options. The relocation issue may be serious enough to cause a prospective librarian to eliminate the profession from consideration. Schools of library and information science, recognizing geographic limitations as a potential obstacle to recruiting students, are working to address this issue. For prospective librarians for whom relocation is problematic, or for whom a geographically convenient program is not the best choice, the flexibility of distance education may be an attractive alternative to a traditional, in-residence program.[3] These programs may also facilitate the transition to librarianship from a previous career, creating possibilities for a more gradual change; for example, the student might decide to remain in a current position while taking a part-time distance program in LIS.

Mature individuals returning to school after a long absence may need extra initial support and encouragement as they reenter the academic environment. They may also need training in the use of technological tools, which will be necessary for them both as students and as practitioners. Programs seeking to attract mature students will need to anticipate and address these concerns. As tools are developed to support delivery of excellent academic preparation for librarianship in a flexible way, the potential barriers (especially geography and time) will be reduced for individuals considering a midlife career change to librarianship.

PRIOR EXPERIENCE

There are many potential paths to librarianship. Lawyers, scientists, business executives, teachers, parents returning to the workforce after taking time to raise children, and many others are graduate students in LIS today. Some may find their way into academic reference in areas where their prior experience is closely related to their area of practice in their new profession, where the connection between the "old" and the "new" is fairly direct. For others, their break with the past may be more complete, and the value of their prior experience may be more difficult to establish. In the context of recruiting excellent candidates for vacant positions in academic reference, seemingly "unrelated" experience might prove highly valuable in practice, particularly when complemented by the depth of professional library experience of the existing reference staff. Depending upon the individual circumstances, this broader background might well be an attractive alternative to the often-required year or more of "professional experience." Administrators faced with the challenge of finding the best possible fit for a given vacancy might want to revisit the issue of experience requirements to permit consideration of candidates from the pool of midlife career changers with newly minted library degrees.

"ANSWER PEOPLE" WANTED

There are probably as many reasons for changing careers at midlife as there are people who do it, and as many compelling stories of success or failure. The process involves soul searching, risk taking, trading the security of the known for the possibilities of the unknown. Librarianship should be a tempting alternative career for "answer people" toiling in other areas of endeavor. The professional library associations should make it a priority to increase public awareness of careers in librarianship. And current practitioners and administrators should cultivate an open-minded attitude about who and where prospective librarians might be, and strive for the institutional flexibility to welcome their diverse backgrounds and experiences.

NOTES

1. An excellent example from the current professional literature is Beverly P. Lynch and Kimberley Robles Smith, "The Changing Nature of Work in Academic Libraries," *College & Research Libraries* 62:5 (September 2001): 407–20. Many of the authors' observations would be easily "translated" into useful informational literature for prospective librarians. Another helpful, informative article is Candace R. Benefiel, Jeannie P. Miller, and Diana Ramirez, "Baseline Subject Competencies for the Academic Reference Desk," *Reference Services Review* 25:1 (Spring 1997): 83–93. An example of one effort in the direction of a "one-stop shopping" resource for information about careers in librarianship is a website created by students at the Syracuse University School of Information Studies. It is called "Librarians in the 21st Century," and may be found at http://istweb.syr.edu/21stcenlib/index.html.

2. Martha Gould, "Libraries in the New Millennium and Political Realities," *PNLA Quarterly* 66:1 (Fall 2001): 6.

3. See Norman Oder, "LIS Distance Ed Moves Ahead," *Library Journal* 126:16 (1 October 2001): 54–57. For further reading, a bibliography of documents related to distance education in LIS has been created by the LEEP Program at the Graduate School of Library and Information Science at the University of Illinois at Urbana-Champaign. It may be viewed at http://www.lis.uiuc.edu/gslis/degrees/leep _bib.html.

37

Academic Librarians as Caring Knowledge Managers

Are We There Yet?

Wendy Tan

Back in the "dark" ages, when automation still sounded like science fiction to the general public, the ranking of an academic library on the organizational chart of a university was jokingly termed "a child out of wedlock," which could be translated as: Its existence cannot be denied, but it would hardly occupy a pivotal place. Due to a lack of firm support by university authorities, the progress of library service and the status of academic librarians were nothing but stagnant. Nevertheless, as the sole keeper of research resources on the campus along with librarians' profound knowledge and dedication, libraries continued to play a vital role in students' pursuit of academic excellence. Our contributions were widely recognized and appreciated by students and faculty alike.

As the world evolved, automation came on to the horizon of civilization. It made an impact on our daily life at a pace faster than anyone could imagine. The concept of automation has always been the epitome of human intelligence, and the most significant contribution toward this journey is the advent of computers. It is quite understandable why this era has been labeled the "computer age."

Most of our wonderful inventions throughout history seem to have derived from a single aim—to ease human burdens. We wanted machines that could push, pull, lift and turn without getting tired. We wanted gadgets that would perform repetitive and tedious work. We wished for appliances that were capable of performing tasks that were beyond human intelligence and speed limits. We wanted information to be available to us at a split second. The list could go on and on. Well, it is safe to say that our prayers have been partially answered in this computer age. At the very least, library work has been "face lifted" under the auspices of automation.

Since countless publications have documented how automation has revolutionized library operations, it is not necessary to dwell on this topic in detail here. In summary, we have benefited from the products of science and new technologies such as online catalogs; computerized information retrievals; electronic data transmission; information sharing; and electronic mail. In addition, there are strong indications that the upper limits of new innovations are still far from being reached.

There is a question frequently raised, whether librarians and patrons in general embraced library automation wholeheartedly. Even though the answer to this question may be a definite yes, we must still examine some of the pitfalls that are associated with this changing library landscape.

When it comes to pinpointing the drawbacks of library automation, the first thing that comes to people's minds must be: computer downtime; computer glitches; high cost; user unfriendliness, and so on. However, for those of us who are involved in and dedicated to servicing patrons for their information needs, our concerns are somewhat geared toward another direction.

A great number of academic librarians have noted that the process of library automation actually signified the end of an era when technique of library use was treated as a required course for higher education. An article published in the *Chronicle of Higher Education* recently stated that nowadays college students go to the library not through a door, but via telephone lines. In other words, the downhill trend of library users on college campuses has been manifested throughout the country since Web surfing became a fad of information searching. The implications of this chilling fact could very well mean departmental budget reductions or even elimination of library jobs.

While this gloomy future does not sound foreign to librarians who have been battling many changes, the struggle we are now facing in this Internet world may be more poignant than ever. Students are becoming an ally to school administrations in a battle against the support of library services, since at this stage in most students' views, the importance of libraries is somewhat like "the eyes of the blind; or the ears of the deaf."

In reality, the threat of machines eliminating human intervention penetrates almost every facet of our society. The nightmare that we will lose control of our career objectives or destiny will come to light to haunt us if we succumb to the power of automation instead of making the best use of its advantages.

So, looking ahead to the future, will our profession flourish or vanish under this rapidly changing wind? From my viewpoint, it is absolutely not the time to prepare an epilogue for an illustrious career. I see a brilliant future ahead.

I am a born believer that the value of human touch is irreplaceable. Although it is very true that patrons can retrieve a wealth of information from the Net without librarians' assistance, oftentimes, as I have witnessed, patrons were delighted to know a caring human being was there ready to render services. Face-to-face interaction is still very appealing, and nonverbal exchange of body language always carries meaning. Meanwhile, there are certain qualities of manual toil that cannot be reproduced by machines. Therefore, automation and the World Wide Web cannot take our places in the information world. With human caring as a base, we also have to take different measures appropriate for the challenges we face in the course of providing information to our patrons.

"Here today, gone tomorrow" is how technologies are upon us at present. To take on the battle imposed by the "omnipotent" Internet, we have to equip ourselves with a mentality of keeping abreast of current developments. That sense of stagnancy of yesteryears should be gone with the retirement of library card catalogs! If our knowledge does not get updated, then our résumés perhaps will have to be updated to get out of academic librarianship.

Furthermore, to make a difference with regard to the Internet as the premiere information providers, we have to advance and present ourselves as *Knowledge Managers*. Simply put, we have the capability and technical know-how to transform libraries into one-stop shopping centers for all information retrievals. We are the knowledge consultants that help our patrons navigate through and utilize the tremendous resources available through variant channels. Technology may have transformed the process of information gathering and retrieval, but it has also grown into almost unmanageable, beastly proportions. It is up to us to tame it and to manage it. We apply our knowledge and skills to screen and group information to make the process of information searching more precise and efficient for our patrons.

What will the future hold for academic librarianship? Success? Failure? The choice rests upon our vision and determination. As an old saying goes, "Sometimes failure occurs because we did not know how close we were to success." A true pioneer sees opportunity in every calamity. Therefore, we must never give up the opportunity to make a difference toward our profession. With growing needs and appreciation for the professionals whose hearts are dedicated to "taking care" of their fellow human beings, academic librarianship is and shall always be the jewel in the crown of higher education.

REFERENCES

Bender, David. "Knowledge management: there is more to information than access." 2001. Available online at http://www.sla.org/pr/pbusiness.html.

"Knowledge managers and libraries." 2001. Available online at http://www.libraryhq.com/knowledge.html.

Dougherty, Richard M. "The computer revolution in research libraries," *The Courier (UNESCO)* 38 (Feb. 1985): 26–27.

Euster, Joanne. "Coping with changing times," *Wilson Library Bulletin* 69 (May 1995): 60–61.

Himmelfarb, Gertrude. "Revolution in the library," *The American Scholar* 66 (Spring 1997): 197–204.

Montanelli, Dale S., Stenstrom, Patricia. *People come first: user-centered academic library service* (Chicago: ACRL, 1999).

Nemmer, S. *Librarianship: a changing profession* (Tallahassee, FL: Florida State University, 1998).

Reed, Sally Gardner. *Creating the future: essays on librarianship in an age of great change* (Jefferson, NC: McFarland, 1996).

Rehman, Sajjad ur. *Preparing the information professional: an agenda for the future* (Westport, CT: Greenwood Press, 2000).

Shatz, Bruce. "Information retrieval in digital libraries: bringing search to the Net," *Science* 275 (Jan. 17, 1997): 327–34.

Srikantaiah, Kanti (ed.). *Knowledge management for the information profession* (Information Today, 2000).

Young, Peter. "Librarianship: a changing profession," *Daedalus* 125 (Fall, 1996): 103–25.

38

Electronic Resources Librarians in the 21st Century

Eleanor L. Lomax

The electronic resources librarian became one of the buzzword titles in libraries toward the end of the 20th century. There appeared to be a growing belief or, at least, a perception that the "electronic" or "online" resource was one that could not be handled using the standard procedures used for other formats. Unarguably, electronic resources did present new issues at multiple points in their progress through the normal workflow of "request-evaluate-purchase-provide." Many libraries found, for one reason or another, that some segments of the staff did not have the capabilities or desire to work with this rapidly emerging format and the new issues it was generating. Consequently, there developed a demand for librarians who were interested in taking on the challenges involved in the acquisition, provision and management of the electronic resources.

What will become of this electronic resources librarian as the 21st century marches on? Will it continue as a distinct position? Will there continue to be "job security" for those currently holding the title? Will it be a reasonable career goal for new librarians or for those seeking a change? Are there new factors or conditions that might define, redefine or possibly eliminate the position in this new century?

Conversations with electronic resources librarians and a look at recent job advertisements and descriptions provide a glimpse of what electronic resources librarians are doing in libraries today. Both commonalities and individualistic approaches are seen with regard to requirements and responsibilities and even the position title. Similar responsibilities included in these are such things as dealing with licensing issues, gathering and maintaining usage data, Web page development and maintenance, evaluating electronic products, and acting as a liaison within and outside of the library. Other responsibilities appear to depend on individual library needs. These include original and adaptive cataloging, training and developing user documentation, managing acquisition and fiscal control, and implementing initiatives in support of distance education.

What are library administrators looking for in the people who will fill these positions? All the standard requirements and experience needed for any librarian position are reflected in these recent job postings (i.e., highly motivated; team-oriented; excellent oral, written and interpersonal skills; problem-solving skills, etc.). And, yes, the MLS or MLIS is still the degree required. Experience and skills, specific to the position, most often listed as needed and/or preferred include: HTML/XML; library software applications, license and contract negotiation; knowledge of electronic academic publishing; development of standards, policies and procedures; database searching; effective training skills; and knowledge of copyright. In some cases, more sophisticated technical skills and experience are required. These include TCP/IP, Z39.50, scanning, graphics, Dublin Core, metadata, digital photography, MS Access/database management systems, computer hardware, and client/server applications. If the position is combined with other duties, the experience and requirements vary by individual library and can include such things as cataloging electronic resources, collection development, library instruction and reference.

What titles are libraries assigning to the position, other than electronic resources librarian? Titles encountered include: Electronic Resources Access Librarian; Instruction/Electronic Resources Librarian; Electronic Services/Systems Librarian; Serials & Electronic Collection Librarian; Electronic Resources Catalog Librarian; Electronic & Information Resources Librarian; and Electronic Resources/Serials Acquisitions Librarian. Possibly, some of these are indicative of a trend away from one centralized position and toward dispersing responsibilities within the various departments of the library. Those that appear to be "combination" titles may simply reflect the economic mandate to "do more with less," an all too familiar and not unusual occurrence in libraries.

A relevant article entitled "Where are Librarians Headed in the 21st Century?" by D.Y. Wu examines the qualifications that library administrators are looking for as delineated in job advertisements and job descriptions. The list of desired qualifications is very similar to those mentioned above, yet the examination covered all types of library positions, not just electronic resources librarians. With regard to titles being used in librarianship, Wu's findings reveal some ". . . more 'current' terms, such as information processing consultant, Web administrator and consultant, coordinator of instructional technology, computer services librarian, information literacy librarian, infrastructure technology institute information specialist, outreach librarian, distance learning librarian and Internet surfer."[1] These findings seem indicative of the ever-increasing presence of technology and electronic resources in libraries today and the need for all librarians to be well prepared to function in that environment.

Where the electronic resources librarian fits in the library's organization is also variable. Most often this position is a part of the Reference Department, but not always. There are cases where this librarian is a member of the Cataloging, Serials, Systems, Technical Services or Access Services Departments. It is not unusual to hear those in the position relate that they were recruited from within the ranks or that their position simply evolved over time. Most probably, this resulted when the gradual shift to electronic resources became rapid and overwhelming. Interested librarians already familiar and knowledgeable regarding the library and its electronic history were "in the right place, at the right time."

What specifically will electronic resources librarians be doing over the next few decades, at least? Even a cursory review of the literature from the late 1990s to the present will yield a multitude of predictions, advice and notes of caution for libraries and librarians vis-à-vis the 21st century. In 1997, Carlen Ruschoff identified what he felt were the most important issues for academic libraries as the new century approached. These were ". . . defending the library budget, preserving materials, and providing access to a growing number of materials."[2] These are not novel issues. Electronic resources afford unique opportunities of dealing with these issues in new ways.

Karl Bridges, in his recent article in *American Libraries*, exhorts librarians in general to be more cautious in how they use technology and not to substitute it in place of service. In his opinion, many libraries have not adequately planned and considered all of the issues involved in their rapid adoption of technology and electronic resources. Bridges feels that there needs to be a balance between technological knowledge and traditional library practice. He does, however, point out that in many cases academic libraries have responded to mandates from colleges and universities that are driven by a competitive market.[3]

In his 2001 article, "The Virtual University: Organizing to Survive in the 21st Century," Dees Stallings predicts ". . . that most communicating and learning in the future will be done at a distance."[4] Despite the predictions of some that computers will surpass humans in areas of intelligence, Stallings believes that the human being will still be the dominant presence in higher education, whether it be in person or online. He and others do foresee an even greater demand for anytime-anywhere education that will result in technologically mediated instruction being a major component in the higher education of the future. These are only three articles, yet they reflect much of what is being written and discussed at this time.

It appears evident that some responsibilities and activities of electronic resources librarians will remain constant. But, will it be the electronic resources librarian performing them? More and more librarians now have the technology skills needed and new librarians coming out of library school are well prepared. This may result in a return to the traditional. The electronic resource will be handled just like any other resource. Specifically, serials librarians will manage electronic journals; acquisition librarians will handle purchasing; collection development librarians will evaluate and select, and so on. There are some responsibilities that are shared already and will need to continue in that vein; for example, access to the resources may be provided in both the catalog and on Web pages with different individuals responsible for each; copyright, fair use and licensing are all interrelated, yet need to involve many individuals.

What might the 21st century hold in store for electronic resources librarians? If the position continues as a distinct one, responsibilities may lessen, shift or change focus.

Those currently holding these positions are well aware of the many problems and persistent issues. They may find themselves now and in the future better able to concentrate their efforts on addressing some of the more critical questions (e.g., usage statistics, preservation and archiving, providing access to materials and services remotely, and creating effective management systems for electronic products).

Unfortunately, this new century has begun with a downturn in the economy that is making it necessary for libraries to make some difficult choices after a number of relatively comfortable years. How does one defend the expenditure of large sums of money for resources that are not physically on the shelf? How do libraries choose one product over another when cuts are mandated? Usage statistics are one of the vitally important tools to good library management, especially so when making decisions about electronic resources. It is an area in which there is still much to be done.

Some publishers and producers of electronic resources do not or claim they cannot supply usage statistics. Others supply them but not necessarily according to any standard format or in such a way as to be helpful in demonstrating a product's worth. In these times of rapid change when so many are having difficulty understanding what libraries are composed of, useful data can go a long way in justifying funding for library services and materials. Electronic resources librarians have traditionally been responsible for gathering and managing the statistics that are available. This aspect of the job should be expected to persist. As other responsibilities shift, work in this area may be expanded to include more in-depth statistical analysis and interpretation, more communication with publishers/vendors and more proactive initiatives within the professional associations and organizations in order to bring about standards in usage reporting.

Preservation and archiving of electronic resources is of major concern when considering electronic resources. Right now, there is no system in place to protect electronic content. Libraries have been forced into situations of licensing material rather than buying it outright. In many cases, once a library decides to no longer pay for and license a product, it has no access to the material it once made available. Historically, publishers have not been responsible for the archiving of their publications and they still do not see it as their role. Traditionally, that role belonged to libraries. Because of the opportunities afforded by electronic access, libraries find that they are able to offer vast quantities of information never before available to their users. There have been some archiving initiatives, JSTOR probably among the most recognized. JSTOR and other initiatives, although commendable, do not as yet fill the archiving and preservation needs posed by the ever-expanding electronic environment. Libraries cannot possibly afford to individually archive this material and will need to enter into and contribute to group-wide efforts. Otherwise, they will find it very difficult to provide continual access to resources they once supplied. Historical access to materials is a bedrock principle in librarianship and is something that has been neglected in recent years.

If learning at a distance is to be the norm in this century, it should then be anticipated that library services available remotely will also be the norm. Currently, academic libraries are making more and more of their resources and services available from outside of the library and the trend will need to continue. It is not unreasonable to foresee this same trend also becoming standard in school and public libraries. Home schooling is already a significant factor in how these libraries make resources available. It can certainly be expected that public and private educational institutions will be looking at new ways to reach students using technological advances. If learning from a distance truly does become more common-place, libraries will need to find creative and flexible means of delivering their services and materials in order to ensure equal access to needed information.

For individual libraries, managing all the various aspects of electronic resources has been an imposing task. Hopefully, electronic resources librarians or their counterparts will have more time and the empowerment to construct systems that will include information on publishers/vendors, financial aspects, access information, license rights and limitations, copyright restrictions, statistics information, and other data deemed important to the institution. Ideally, this management system would be made available to library staff with access to relevant information also being available to the library's users. Librarians who are experienced and familiar with designing and creating database management systems will continue to play an important role.

Technology has progressed at a rapid pace and there is no reason to believe that this will not continue. The future, undoubtedly, will introduce some yet unimaginable technological advancements affecting the way information is used and delivered. Librarians, as always, will need to be willing to keep pace and to take the initiative when it comes to planning and managing the use of new technologies in their libraries. The challenge will be to maintain the traditional values of the profession and preserve a system that has contributed to the social, political, intellectual and technological advancements of the past century. For this we need librarians with communication and critical thinking skills who are committed to preserving the historical underpinnings of the profession.

The electronic resources librarian of today is well positioned to take an active part in resolving these current issues and participating in the implementation of ventures still to come. New position titles for some of the same responsibilities will continue to be created, hopefully to better reflect what individuals are doing and not simply to impress. People capable and willing to work with electronic resources and the myriad issues and methods of delivery will continue to be in high demand. For those who are willing, there are exciting times ahead.

NOTES

1. Yuhfen Diana Wu, "Where are Librarians Headed in the 21st Century?" *Journal of Educational Media & Library Sciences* 37 (2000): 349–57.

2. Carlsen Ruschoff, "What are the Most Important Issues Confronting Academic Librarianship as we Approach the 21st Century?" *The Journal of Academic Librarianship* 23 (1997): 321–22.

3. Karl Bridges, "Why Traditional Librarianship Matters," *American Libraries* 32 (2001): 52–54.

4. Dees Stallings, "The Virtual University: Organizing to Survive in the 21st Century," *The Journal of Academic Librarianship* 27 (2001): 3–14.

39

Competition in
the Library

David M. Bynog

The future of librarianship can be simply summed up: competition. Librarians must learn to focus on self-promotion and review resource allocation in an increasingly competitive field. To perform this, they should keep the basic principles of librarianship and merge them with the changing face of knowledge, information, and society. The basic skills needed for future academic librarians are already in place. Organization, accessibility, and preservation form a solid base of core components for libraries, but increased technology has thrown a wild card into the mix. Technology has not changed what libraries do; it merely changes the way in which we do it. It has allowed such ventures as online cataloging, enhanced resource sharing, and greater ease in obtaining materials. However it has also created a greater avenue for information and a greater demand for speed and accuracy. Librarians must find new ways to incorporate their skills and knowledge and apply them to an evolving field. If libraries want to continue to thrive, they must learn to be more competitive.

Librarians must understand the importance of a library's greatest commodity: information. While librarians have traditionally held a prominent place in the informational food chain, the explosion of information in recent years has made the efforts to harness it an insurmountable task. Still noted for their organization and access to information, librarians face an increase in interest and competition from the business sector. Many librarians debate the relative worth of a bookstore, a search engine, or an online business compared to a librarian's expertise, but the reality is that these competitors are indeed drawing patrons from the library and serving some of their needs. While they may never prove to be a replacement for a library, they are proving adept at performing some of the same functions and needs for their customers. And if a regular library patron can find a nice, comfortable area to study at the local café while enjoying his bagel and latte, he may not be a regular library patron forever.

For libraries to effectively compete they need to either perform a service better, give up on a particular function that they can't perform better, or work with the competition. One area that libraries are actively addressing is their function as a study area. Traditionally the heart and soul of a university campus, the library finds competition from other areas, from dorm rooms to bookstores. Since patrons have greater freedoms in choice of study and leisure reading areas, they are increasingly requesting amenities such as eating spaces, comfortable seating, and extended hours in libraries. Many libraries, both public and academic, are listening to their patrons and redesigning library space with trendy couches and cyber cafes. While some libraries can choose to compete for students by providing better study opportunities, they can also opt out of competition, providing minimal study areas. Libraries with heavy concentrations of commuting students and distance education students may find it better to divert resources to off-campus users rather than maintain study areas that no one wants to use. Belief in the traditional, core values of librarianship does not mean clinging to one model, rather it means understanding your user population and being adaptable to meet their needs.

The loss of traditional functions for libraries may be a hard pill for some to swallow, but asking libraries to work together with their competition also creates strong emotions. This is particularly strange given the harmonious relationships that libraries have been forging between themselves. Libraries have increasingly been forming partnerships with other libraries, in spite of being direct competitors. Consortial agreements not only give libraries more negotiating power with publishers and vendors, but research sharing also allows many libraries to better manage limited funds.

While libraries are competitors between themselves they also form natural allies, typically sharing traditional goals and principles. However, if libraries want to truly expand and remain competitive, they should seek out partnerships in other areas. Outsourcing of traditional functions, such as cataloging, is one type of partnership that libraries have participated in, to the chagrin of many in the profession, but there are other avenues. This may mean working with bookstores by sending patrons over to use newly published materials, persuading software stores to start hiring persons with an MLS, or even sending patrons over to the local video store and subsidizing the cost of a DVD rental. Far-fetched, possibly, but if libraries incur the costs of obtaining materials via interlibrary loan, what are the differences in renting materials from local businesses to loan out to their patrons? The logistics may be difficult but no more difficult than the work of many in national library organizations or local committees. Libraries and librarians can either learn to adapt and seek out creative solutions to changes in society or find themselves going the way of the dinosaurs.

While librarians may understand the added value they can provide to patrons, they must work harder than before to prove it. With increased demands on time, many patrons want things quick and easy. This is not a new phenomenon, but with the relative ease of finding information available via the Internet, they are increasingly settling on what is most convenient. Blanket solutions may not be effective for every library, and deciding on which areas of service to cut back on or enhance depends on local issues. The truth is that the rapid changes in society's wants and needs are having a significant impact on how and when patrons want their information. With these changes librarianship must change to meet those needs or others will, and are, moving in to fill in the gaps. Pleading to an empty library that you can provide the best resources, rather than merely sufficient resources freely available on the Internet is not likely to have much of an effect. With increased alternatives for information librarians must learn to gain a competitive edge and promote the added values that they provide to information.

40

Qualities of a 21st-Century Librarian

Necia Parker-Gibson

Although the world in which librarianship exists has changed radically in the last few decades, the qualities needed in new librarians are much the same as those of previous generations of the profession. However, several of them may be needed in greater measure because of technological, political or economic challenges. These qualities include the following.

CURIOSITY

A librarian should be at least a *little* interested in everything, should read a little, often, in professional literature and in other areas, and should be aware of the world around him or her, even as the world becomes more complex. Learn and understand a little (or a lot) about your community, especially if you've moved in order to be employed, as happens to many new librarians.

COMMUNICATION SKILLS

Each librarian must have communication skills that will allow him or her to negotiate a contract, a question, or a quarrel with someone across the desk, across town or across the globe, by telephone, by e-mail, or face to face. Asynchronous reference service and "chat reference" is more and more common, so being able to negotiate a question by written communication is that much more important, and distance education students must be helped by mail, video, telephone, or e-mail. Jobbers are found across the country, and publishers are found around the world.

A SOLID, BROAD EDUCATION

Not every librarian needs to be classically trained, but the more one knows about a variety of subjects, the better a librarian one can become. A second language, or more than one, is always useful, and aids in cataloging and reference work alike. Even a few words or phrases of Spanish, German or Italian, not to mention Japanese or Arabic, will go far as our communities become more diverse.

The notion of a broad education includes a willingness to continue one's education, both to acquire that useful second master's degree, which is often required in academic libraries for promotion and tenure, and to ground oneself in the subject(s) for which one is, or becomes, responsible. GraceAnne DeCandido, in her 1996 commencement speech, "Ten Graces for New Librarians" delivered to the School of Information Science at SUNY Albany, said:

You have your degree, but you make your education every day. . . . Realize that your degree is only the beginning. The world of librarianship is unimaginably different now from what it was in 1972 when I got my MLS from the late, lamented Columbia University; in fact, it is unimaginably different from what it was five years ago when I got my first e-mail address; or two years ago when I first heard the words, 'World Wide Web.' Keep learning stuff; as a librarian, you are in a unique position to do so.

DeCandido is one of the mentors-at-a-distance I, and most likely many others, claim in librarianship. She writes well, and often, and is a great advocate for librarians and libraries.

Learn new software. Find a small toolkit, and a flashlight, for your desk drawer and learn to troubleshoot hardware, including printers, and make do with what you have. Don't work on machines that are plugged in, but stay plugged-in to your profession through journals and discussion lists.

TOLERANCE FOR CHANGE

Libraries are changing, willy-nilly. Either we accept and promote change, or we will find ourselves in other occupations. E-books and e-journals are here to stay, barring catastrophes that destroy the Web world. Purchasing through consortia and approval plans is now the norm rather than the exception. The academic library, which in the public mind was quiet, dim, and full of sweatered professors and studious coeds, is now full of computers, music, paper recycling, discussion, and often, food and drink. The professors are wearing fleece and jeans, or suits, depending on the discipline, and the coeds are working away on their laptops while they listen to CDs or MP3s. The public library that was the dusty haven for after-school study has hustle and bustle, computers, and homework help; latch-key kids, literacy groups, homeless people, and political groups often find themselves at home in the library. Special libraries will be open more hours and tackle more projects in more different ways, than ever.

APPRECIATION/TOLERANCE

See also tolerance for change. The professional ranks will need to be more inclusive of persons from other races, creeds, sexual orientations, and socioeconomic backgrounds. Not everyone will be, or should be, of the same learning style, management style, or professional style. If we only hire those who look (or walk, talk, think, manage) like "us," as has been the tendency in this and a number of other professions, then we tend to close our profession to those who are not like us, and we lose creativity and diversity that would be to our profession's and our readers' benefit. For more on this subject, see the writings of Kathleen de la Pena McCook, among others.

FLEXIBILITY

Flexibility in librarianship entails the ability to take on different tasks, within the same day, or even within the same hour, and not lose one's equilibrium. The odds are that staffing levels per library will continue to decline. The chances are that the job that one was hired for is not the job one is doing, if one has been there longer than a year. This means that those who continue in the profession will have to develop new skills and adapt old ones; be flexible enough to realize that library school is to library work as making a sandwich is to creating a buffet for fifty people—it's much more rewarding but also much more complex and often stressful. Be willing to change professions if librarianship proves not to be your niche.

A STUBBORN PRAGMATICISM

Librarians of the future will need to be able to continue the awful balancing act of staying within the budget and satisfying the needs of the readers, without driving themselves crazy over missed opportunities. Although in many professions, what is decided may not seem to matter in a hundred years, in ours, especially in relation to collections, it may. None of us can afford to let this fact freeze us. As one librarian I know often says, "Rules are not as important as knowing when and if to break them." Sometimes, we will have to buy books; sometimes, buy software instead of books; sometimes buy hardware instead of collecting volumes, even if the publications may never be available to the library again. As a result, we must continue to cultivate networks, consortial relationships and other reciprocal relationships, and continue to consider our collections within the context of what we have in common with other libraries, and what we have that is unique. Collection development, which for me, ten years ago in library school, emphasized book purchases and knowing the needs of my immediate readers, is really collection *management,* including print, e-resources, and new formats. Weeding and repair-or-replace decisions have to continue to balance purchases, especially in a climate where shelf space is costly and less available, and electronic purchases will be likely to outweigh print.

DON'T BECOME TOO PRAGMATIC

Librarians will have to continue to be willing to collect materials that will only appeal to a few readers, and materials that may offend some readers. The political climate after the World Trade Center disaster may seem to preclude anything but a sturdy patriotism, but we must continue to support and collect alternative content, opinions, religions, and politics. A good library should have something in the collection to offend everyone.

A GENIAL WILLINGNESS TO SPEND OTHER PEOPLE'S MONEY

Librarians will need to be able to spend donations and other endowments without losing sleep over each dollar, or even each thousand dollars. Appropriate care must be taken, but second-guessing ourselves is out.

A GENIAL WILLINGNESS TO ASK FOR MONEY

Librarians will need to be willing and able to help generate and expand their endowments, donations, and other monies, as public monies will continue to be in short supply. Shake hands, join the Rotary Club (public librarians, especially), be visible on campus, or involved in whatever organization is its parallel for your situation, and be willing to put your needs forward.

A STUBBORN DETERMINATION TO BE AN ADVOCATE FOR LIBRARIES AND LIBRARIANS

See my comment about DeCandido; if we are not our own advocates through involvement in issues, professional organizations, and our institutions, to a great extent, no one else will be.

AN INDEPENDENT INCOME OR A LOW DEBT LOAD

Although salaries have improved in some cases, librarianship is not commonly a profession in which to get wealthy.

A SENSE OF HUMOR

Librarians are better off with a robust sense of humor, as well as a good measure of humility. At the end of the day, don't take yourself, or your job, too seriously.

41

The More Things Change in Academe, the More They Need to Stay the Same

Karen Fischer

What kind of people will become college librarians in the future? No doubt they will have highly technical skills. Yet, those skills identified as technical and specialized change over time. I can remember when being able to put a 5 1/4-inch floppy disc into a computer and change directories at the C: prompt was a highly technical skill reserved for the electrical engineering graduate. (They weren't called computer scientists then.) Is there anyone who uses a computer now who can't put a disc of some kind into a drive and access the information on it? So, what was once a specialized technical skill is now considered both widespread and basic.

In our field today, good people learn what they need to know technically, not just once, but several times over the course of a career as technology and the need change. Will the future be any different for our profession in that regard? Perhaps instead of focusing on important technical skills they should have, we need to focus on on what key innate qualities future academic librarians need to bring to the field. The standard list appears in position announcements over and over: curiosity, the

ability to learn new skills, an appreciation for the field, good communication skills, the ability to work in both a team environment and independently, a sympathetic understanding of academe, being service
oriented, and so on.

I believe a college library needs people with a variety of backgrounds
and skills. It is that very mixture that makes an institution a vibrant place
capable of adapting to a changing environment. Suppose a new college
library was being established in the future and the staff was being assem-
bled for the first time. What if famous people from the past were magically
resurrected, acquired the MLS in its future iteration so they had the technical skills and standard theories of their day, and were hired to staff this
new library? What if the following people were part of this new library's
staff: Susan B. Anthony, Barbara McClintock, Charles Darwin, Arthur C.
Clark, Harry Truman, Katherine Graham, Eleanor Roosevelt and Barbara
Jordan. What strengths would they bring to the mix of staff?

Susan B. Anthony worked for the better part of her adult lifetime to
accomplish a goal she never reached. Wouldn't you think eventually she
would have come to realize the hopelessness of ever getting the right to
vote for women? Yet she did not abandon her vision. Our future library
needs a visionary.

And then there was Barbara McClintock, who got her Ph.D. in the 1920s
and never secured a good professional position, but doggedly pursued
her genetic research on corn plants anyway. Her ideas were dismissed as
wrong by her peers. When faced with being ostracized because her own
observations contradicted the standard knowledge of her day, she had
enough faith in herself to stay the course. Eventually she was awarded
the Nobel prize for her research on "jumping genes." Our future library
needs someone who can accurately observe and reach accurate conclusions, not based on what is sacred cow knowledge but on what is.

Charles Darwin was an original thinker. While he built on the knowledge of his day, especially that of the emerging field of geology, and had
read Malthus' *An Essay on the Principle of Population*, he synthesized theories of these other fields with his personal natural history observations
on the *Beagle* and came up with the mechanism for evolution. Alfred Rus-
sel Wallace read Lyell and Malthus and Darwin's account of the *Beagle*
journey before he too came up with the idea of natural selection some
years later. They shared amiably the claim of thinking up natural selection
to explain what they saw in the world around them. Our future library
needs those who can synthesize ideas and observations from a variety of
fields and extrapolate their relevance for college libraries.

Arthur C. Clarke is given credit for first publishing as science fiction technological accomplishments that later came to be fact. He has shown an uncanny ability to extrapolate where science and technology might lead us. Our future library needs a futurist to help it anticipate change.

Harry Truman and Katherine Graham both had greatness thrust upon them. Both suffered the death of the one in charge, one a president, the other a husband. Both came out of the shadows into the glare of the sun, rose to the occasion, made tough decisions and provided undoubted leadership. In their prime, they also shared a knowledge of people and of how politics and influence work. Our future library needs those who have a sense of what is possible, can courageously navigate the land mines along the way and can get the job done.

Barbara Jordan, the congresswoman from Texas, was known far and wide as a gifted, eloquent and persuasive speaker. She was the first woman and first African-American to give a keynote address at a major political party national convention. Our future library could have no better spokesperson.

Eleanor Roosevelt, as the U.S. ambassador to the United Nations, forged a coalition of people of diverse views that made it possible for the United Nations to pass the Universal Declaration of Human Rights. Without her considerable powers of persuasion, that statement might not have passed when it did. Our future library needs a consummate diplomat.

For a couple of thousand years, technology and culture changed slowly. In the present and most likely in the foreseeable future, that pace has accelerated. Change is the norm and will continue to be. Technology will continue to morph and technical knowledge will always be in demand. Yet, the more things change, the more they need to stay the same. When it comes to staffing the library, the visionary, the researcher, the original thinker, the futurist, the practical politician, the diplomat, and the spokesperson have always been important to college libraries. If college libraries are to remain relevant to their clientele, they must continue to adapt to current and future needs. We will continue to need librarians with a variety of personal attributes, that together complement one another and provide the library of the future with both stability and the flexibility to survive and prosper in a changing environment.

42

The Joys of
Special Librarianship

Ronald N. Bukoff

Special libraries encompass specialized areas of interest: music, law, medicine, and so on. It is important to emphasize that special librarianship in the new millennium will be different from librarianship in the past. However, as technical aspects change, the underlying philosophy behind special librarianship remains the same.[1] Keeping *au courant* with new research in science, social science, education, and the arts—a handful of "specialties" found in special libraries—and remaining abreast of relevant new technologies has kept the library profession ever changing and evolving.

The librarian entering the field of special librarianship today needs as much technological background and special expertise as possible; but it is only a foundation for a career in the field. A discussion about the need for technological skills is a given and not the focus of this essay. The special librarian of the third millennium needs much more, as do all librarians. Beyond the needs of technology, the librarian needs a battery of useful personality and character traits: a strong sense of individuality, the ability to see the humor in most situations, the strength to react calmly under pressure, and an altruistic interest in helping others. The special librarian who is able to work in a special library emphasizing his area of interest is fortunate, if not blessed.[2] As Lucille Foster Fargo pointed out in 1927:

A person who rides his hobby well finds a place for it in his professional life. It is frequently the steed on which a librarian rides to success, for specialists are demanded in library service. To "know something about everything and everything about something" is the goal.[3]

To explore those necessary survival traits for the 21st century, I have examined the writings of scholars in the field from the early 20th century to see if their advice resonates today. Surprisingly, many of their comments and observations are still applicable and valid. I take as initial inspiration an address, "The Joys of Librarianship," delivered to the New York Public Library Staff Association by Arthur E. Bostwick, librarian of the St. Louis Public Library, on November 26, 1917. Bostwick, as one might surmise, focuses on the positive aspects of the profession: "If librarianship . . . has joys, they are to be found in the perfect adaptation of the worker to the work and that this adaptation is what we must seek, letting the joy come as a by-product—as it surely will."[4]

The special librarian needs thorough training in the library arts—which includes popular conceits such as information literacy, information specialization, information technology, and so forth—as well as exceptional education in his chosen area of specialty. An interest, nay, a love for learning, should be at the core of the modern librarian's personal makeup. W.O. Thompson, president of Ohio State University, addressed this idea in 1900: "To succeed . . . librarianship should command talent of the very highest order. No one should seek such a calling until assured of an abiding interest in learning."[5] Learning and education for the librarian is a major topic for many writers in the field. In 1920, an anonymous author writing in *New York Libraries* advises us: "Every bit of equipment counts in the librarian's favor, and his general preparation should be as well-rounded and extensive as possible."[6] Commenting on special librarianship two years later, Claribel Ruth Barnett recognizes:

A special library is only a part of an institution. As a part of an institution, it is most important that the special library be in harmony with the institution and the librarian should be loyal to its interests. The only excuse for the special library's existence is to help to realize the aims of the institution. The librarian ought to know not only what he is doing but why he is doing it. And he ought to see his work in relation to all the other work of the institution or organization.[7]

This thought is still valid today.

The special library exists to support the work of its parent institution, whether the latter is academic-, public-, or business-connected. And the special librarian serves the needs of the special library. Extra training in the field of study germane to the special library is a must. Libraries have always required subject knowledge, usually in the form of additional academic degrees relevant to the library's specialization. This situation will not change in the future. Current knowledge and ongoing education are benchmarks of special education. Writing in 1922, W.E. Henry agrees: "So, for the future let no one contemplate the profession of librarianship who has not lived long in the presence of culture or scholarship or both."[8] Therefore, the music librarian should have specialized training in music, the art librarian, in art, the law librarian, in law, and so on. This concept was more recently accentuated by Lester Asheim: "The *academic* librarian will have to be highly qualified to be an academic librarian, and not a sort of all-purpose public, school, college, or special library employee. The interchangeable skills are paraprofessional qualifications; the professional's talents are more rigorous and exacting."[9]

I now turn to those personality traits crucial for the survival of the special librarian: individuality, humor, the ability to remain calm under pressure, and altruism. Readers may be surprised about the first, individuality. Individuality arises with the need to be flexible and adaptive to the environment of the special library and its patrons. This environment is ever changing and the librarian must have the internal strength of character to recognize, identify, and resolve the myriad problems that develop, from the small to large. Special librarianship is not for the timid.

Nevertheless, the special librarian can cope with nearly all situations by calling upon a necessary and crucial sense of humor and joy. Most writers on the topic of librarianship ignore this important personality and survival trait. However, Bostwick addresses the topic: "To persons with a sense of humor, work in libraries offers very special joys, which come, according to my view, as an indication that such persons are fitted in some particular way for their task."[10] Humor, laughter, and joy will get the librarian through most of the trials and tribulations that can occur in the course of a normal workday. They also help to combat the librarian's stereotype of the repressed spinster librarian *à la* "Marion the Librarian" from Meredith Willson's *The Music Man*. And, of course, humor provides the ability to react calmly in times of stress. The library is not a safe haven removed from the problems of the world. The library, even the special library, is part and parcel of the world, and the special librarian must cope with the pressures that arise with modern life. They cannot be avoided. This is where humor becomes vital; it provides a useful safety valve for the pressure cooker that is modern society.

Last, but not least in this litany of necessary survival traits, is the desire to help others. Many writers of the early 20th century focus on altruism. As always, Bostwick describes the "joys that come from the librarian's contact with the public. A classic answer when one asks a candidate for librarianship about his qualification is: 'I'm very fond of books.' It might be more to the point if he were able to say, 'I'm very fond of people.'" Writing over a century ago, Thompson is adamant about this characteristic:

[Librarianship] certainly cannot attract to itself the narrow-minded or the selfish. It furnishes no field for the display of those qualities of heart and mind which accompany a love of display, an ambition for power, and others I need not mention. The librarian must be a public servant. . . . All his life and all his work are to be directed toward, and in the interest of, others. This service, too, is of a most intelligent and painstaking sort. It is idle for us to think of such a life as a bed of roses.[11]

Thompson's view still reverberates today. Librarianship is a service to the public, and it is not for the faint of heart. It might be "a bed of roses," but if it is, the roses retain their thorns.

Special librarianship in the third millennium will provide new challenges—personal, intellectual, and technological—to the librarian. But, the profession has always offered many rewards to librarians. An anonymous librarian, writing for the New York State Education Department in 1911, provides a summation: "For one, who . . . has the wish to help and serve others, there is no better field and few in which intelligent work is more needed."[12] Additionally, I would like to tell special librarians of the future: know and love yourself; embrace the joy; develop your intellectual and technological skills to the highest level; and, above all, love your patrons.[13] *Plus ça change, plus c'est la même chose.*

NOTES

1. I would like to thank Marcia Alexander of Magale Library, Centenary College of Louisiana, for perceptive suggestions concerning this essay.

2. The modern reader may freely substitute *she* and *her* in lieu of *he* and *his*.

3. Lucille Foster Fargo, "Preparation for Librarianship," *Journal of the N.E.A.* 16 (1927), 243–45, in *The Library as a Vocation: Reprints of Papers and Addresses*, Harriet Price Sawyer (New York: H.W. Wilson, 1933), 252.

4. Arthur E. Bostwick, "The Joys of Librarianship," *Bulletin of the New York Public Library* (January 1918): 3.

5. W.O. Thompson, "Librarianship as a Profession," *Public Libraries* 5, 10 (1900): 417.

6. "Books and a Vocation," *New York Libraries* 7 (1920), 132–33, in *The Library as a Vocation*, 81.

7. Claribel Ruth Barnett, "Training the Special Librarian," *Special Libraries* 13 (1922), 133–35, in *The Library as a Vocation*, 188.

8. W.E. Henry, *Librarianship: A Profession* (Seattle: University of Washington Press, 1922), 17–18.

9. Lester Alsheim, "Education of Future Academic Librarians," in *Academic Libraries by the Year 2000: Essays Honoring Jerrold Orne*, ed. Herbert Poole (New York: R.R. Bowker, 1977), 136.

10. Bostwick, 12.

11. Thompson, 417.

12. *Librarianship: An Uncrowded Calling* (Albany: New York State Education Department, 1911), 6.

13. If you can't bring yourself to love your patrons, at least try to like them.

43

New Librarians in the 21st Century

The Normalization of Change

Lorena O'English

For the past few decades the profession of librarianship has been characterized as a profession in transition. The question becomes, how long can a state of transition exist without it eventually becoming institutionalized? In what seems to be a paradox, transition becomes the foundation of everyday life and change becomes normalized. New librarians of the 21st century will need to be comfortable with change because that is very likely going to be the environment in which they live out their careers. Librarians do not exist in a vacuum, and the trends of the future will strongly influence the future of the profession.

Given the changes in the profession that will inevitably occur, what qualities will we require of new librarians entering the field? And are they that much different from the skills and characteristics that are expected from librarians of the present? This essay will focus on academic public service librarians as it attempts to develop a sense of some of the things that will very likely be showing up—implicitly or explicitly—in the job descriptions of the future.

THE REFERENCE LIBRARIAN

Most academic public service librarians have reference responsibilities included as part of their job. Just as reference librarianship has changed over the last twenty years, inevitably it will evolve even further in future decades. Trends that will continue into the future include the explosion of electronic resources and the implosion of funding, of course, but also the disintermediation of the librarian-patron relationship, the increase in distance education, and the increase in nontraditional students using the campus library.[1] The traditional ownership of print resources is competing with the new notion of access to electronic resources[2] as campus library patrons demand and increasingly use full-text electronic resources.[3] The new librarian of the 21st century will need to be able to "think outside the box" when it comes to reference service. The current experimentation with digital or virtual reference will no doubt increase, and Martell suggests that this is only the beginning: ". . . librarians must begin to design an imaginative, easily identifiable space in cyberspace as the centrality of the library as a physical phenomenon slowly fades. This does not mean that librarians will be irrelevant or obsolete. It does mean that the services of librarians will be provided most effectively in a virtual environment."[4] He continues, "As the twenty-first century progresses, librarians will deal with users almost exclusively in a virtual environment and face-to-face interchanges will become atypical."[5] While one hopes that this extreme vision of the future does not come to pass, libraries will be looking for new librarians who understand the modalities of working with many different kinds of patrons in a distance relationship, and thriving in an environment of change.

Academic public service librarians understand that teaching is an integral part of their jobs, whether they have a formal "instruction librarian" portfolio or not. Library instruction is becoming increasingly different from the orientation and tool-based instruction of the past. More and more resources means that instruction must cover more and more ground. At the same time the bodies that libraries are responsible to, including university administrations and state legislatures, are increasingly mandating real assessment of student learning that includes library-related areas such as information and technology literacy. And on top of all that, a major change is occurring in the very nature of the college student who is one of the university libraries' main constituents. Increasingly, students ". . . come to college with a far different set of skills, more comfortable with fast-paced change and nonlinear, nonsequential modes of perceiving, thinking and investigating. For them the visual image—not the word—is the primary means of communication and the unifying cultural force" (Roth, 1999, p. 42). This is coupled with a need for skills in evaluating information and knowing when and how to properly cite what they find.[6]

To manage the new realities of instruction, the new librarian of the 21st century will need to be ready to engage in nontraditional methods of library instruction that will keep the attention of students who may not have very long attention spans.[7] These can include techniques such as incorporating active learning, peer learning, and trading the old-school "sage on the stage" for the new-school "guide on the side." Inevitably, however, the new librarian will need to demonstrate proficiency in information literacy instruction, seeing that as the best way to prepare students for the reality of the information environment, both in and beyond their college career. Information literacy has many definitions, but the one from the ALA Presidential Committee on Information Literacy's 1989 Final Report is a good place to start: "To be information literate, a person must be able to recognize when information is needed and have the ability to locate, evaluate, and use effectively the needed information."[8] New librarians will need to cooperate and collaborate with other librarians and discipline faculty to create stand-alone classes linking information literacy and the disciplines, or incorporate IL into the college curriculum. The new librarian will also need to be prepared to plan and engage in ongoing, authoritative assessment to ensure that instruction goals are being achieved.

The previous discussion has focused mainly on librarian skills, rather than personal attributes. Roy Tennant suggests that character traits may be better criteria for identifying potential new hires because ". . . it may be more productive to choose staff who can evolve as the needs of the organization change. Change, after all, is the only constant."[9] Taking this view it can be argued that in the shifting environment that will be 21st-century librarianship a new librarian will need to possess four attributes for survival and success: a customer service orientation, flexibility, strategic thinking, and the capacity for self-renewal.

In an environment where libraries must compete with other sources of information such as the World Wide Web and online library and research services such as Questia and ebrary, customer service becomes increasingly important. At the same time libraries are being pressured to justify their budgets in an era of increasingly dwindling resources. Libraries have not always placed the convenience of the user over the convenience to library employees, as noted by Hannelore Rader: "Limited availability of user survey data indicates that people generally are used to one-stop shopping and expect similar convenience from libraries. Information is wanted quickly, seamlessly and with expert human guidance. These expectations constitute a major challenge for librarians who have usually provided services at their convenience, not always quickly or seamlessly."[10] The individual librarian will play the crucial role as libraries attempt to improve their service delivery. New librarians must recognize that excellence in customer service will be a primary requirement, and that an emphasis on value-added services will be increasingly relevant at all levels of library transactions.

Flexibility will also be a prime characteristic of the new librarian of the future. Flexibility is key to survival in the library of the future. The new librarian must be prepared to cope with change, and not just technological change. As noted above, the student of the 21st century is different from the student of the past, and these differences will undoubtedly become even more prevalent. Technology will change, university library users will change, library missions will change, everything will change—and librarians must adapt, or wither away, defeated on the field, leaving library users to the alternatives of search engines and Ask Jeeves.

Politics is not something generally thought of in the context of librarianship, but the new librarian of the future needs to be prepared to think politically and strategically. As resources constrict, libraries must compete with other campus units to gain their fair share of the pie. Strategic thinking, including the making of strategic alliances, will be required not just from library administrators but from all members of the library staff. Success—including promotion and raises—may very well be tied to how much the individual librarian advances the mission of the library, which in turn must advance the mission of the university.

Clearly the new librarian of the 21st century will be facing a career that will be full of challenges and surprises. The combination of all this suggests that a very important trait for the librarian of the 21st century will be the capacity for self-renewal. Burnout is a major issue in the profession today, and as budgets continue to decline and more and more must be done with less and less, and as technological and societal changes require continuous adjustments, the accompanying stresses will no doubt be a challenge for librarians to cope with. A realistic assessment of one's potential for burnout, coupled with established strategies to reduce that potential, will be necessary if the librarian of the future wants to enjoy a long and rewarding career.[11]

So are there real differences between what we looked for in new librarians ten years ago and what we will look for as we hire in the 21st century? One could make an argument that the skills and characteristics delineated above are all qualities that search committees have always looked for as they review prospective employees' job applications. Nevertheless, it is absolute that the library of the future will not be the same as the library of the past and the present, and those differences will drive the job descriptions of the future. The new library of the 21st century will be completely different from what we have now, just as the 20th-century library is worlds apart from the closed stacks, reference-free academic library of the 19th century. One major consideration is that the new librarian of the future will embody the changes described; that is, she will be a Generation X'er, and then a member of Generation Y, to be supplanted by members of Generation Z and so on down (or up?) the generational alphabet. She will be a product of the transitions of now and the future.

Libraries will change, and librarians will also change. Perhaps, in the end, the most important thing that we will look for in new librarians of the 21st century is the ability to sort through impending changes and separate positive change from negative change. The skills and characteristics mentioned in this essay are all an attempt to identify the qualities that will help the new librarian of the 21st century cope with the change that will be her everyday environment.

NOTES

1. Elizabeth Thomsen, *Rethinking reference: The reference librarian's practical guide for surviving constant change* (New York: Neal-Schuman Publishers, Inc., 1999).

2. Lou Anne Stewart, "Choosing between print and electronic resources: The selection dilemma," *The Reference Librarian* 71 (2000): 79–97.

3. Brad MacDonald and Robert Dunkelberger, "Full-text database dependency: An emerging trend among undergraduate library users?" *Research Strategies* 16 (1998): 301–307.

4. Charles Martell, "The disembodied librarian in the digital age, part II," *College and Research Libraries* 61 (2000): 99–113.

5. Ibid, p. 104.

6. Lorie Roth, "Educating the cut-and-paste generation," *Library Journal* (November 1, 1999): 42–44.

7. Martell, op cit., p. 109.

8. American Library Association Presidential Committee on Information Literacy, Final Report, 1989. Retrieved 8 December 2001, from American Library Association, Association of College and Research Libraries Web site: http://www.ala.org/acrl/nili/ilit1st.html.

9. Roy Tennant, "The most important management decision: Hiring staff for the new millennium," *Library Journal* (February 15, 1998): 102.

10. Hannelore B. Rader, "Information literacy in the reference environment: Preparing for the future," *The Reference Librarian* 71 (2000): 24–33.

11. Janette S. Caputo, *Stress and Burnout in Library Service* (Phoenix, AZ: Oryx Press, 1991), 152.

44

Electric Luddites

Special Collections Librarians Make the Great Leap

Roger C. Adams

In 1993, I sat in the University of Kentucky School of Library and Information Science computer lab waiting seven minutes for a single image to download from the Internet. The picture was coming to me in Lexington from the Vatican Library. I sat—remarkably patient—while I watched the Mosaic Web browser's icon spin and spin. The computer was an IBM 386 and it was one of the best machines in the lab. These were the days when 5 1/4" and 3 1/2" floppy disks still commingled freely. CD-ROMs, MP3s, ZIP drives, Pentium chips and DVDs were not even part of our computing vocabulary.

We were all entranced by the Gopher search engine and many of us carried around little notebooks with handwritten Web addresses to share with cohorts. It was an exciting time to be in library school—if such a thing is actually possible, particularly when we were still learning about Dialog dial-up searching.

The image I waited for so patiently was a single scan of one of the Vatican Library's many illuminated Book of Hours from the Middle Ages. There on the screen for everyone to view was a beautiful scene of the nativity. The greatest part was that we didn't have to go to Italy to see it!

The lapis blue of Mary's cloak and the gold leaf embellishments were brought right to us thousands of miles away in a matter of minutes—albeit an eternity by today's download standards. As I was already in training as a special collections librarian, I thought that the electronic age for that particular breed of librarian would be a long, laborious battle. To my pleasant surprise, special collections librarians—those seemingly immovable objects of traditional paper-based librarianship—have adjusted very quickly and adapted to electronic information delivery.

Many special collections librarians are of an era when the card catalog reigned supreme. Nothing could improve upon those many drawers of tiny, tidy cards organized by title, author, and subject. Any attempt to try to convince one of those "old school" types was a waste of breath. But in a very short time, academic libraries replaced their card catalogs with OPACs. These electronic databases of bibliographic records are faster, easier to use, and offer multiple keyword searches to find more items or refine searches. Today, many libraries' OPACs are Web-based databases which can be searched by anyone in the world with Internet access. However, folks like Nicholson Baker still lament the passing of the traditional card catalog. No one mourns the passing of the Edsel, polyester leisure suits, or New Coke. So why all the fuss over a cumbersome, labor-intensive way of providing access to library materials? The answer is simple: it's an easy target.

Arguments against electronic access for collections from the biblio-Luddites typically come down to this phrase, "Well, technology is good—when it works." My standard reply is, "I like airplanes—when they work." They do have a point, though, particularly when a server which stores the library's OPAC crashes or the power goes out. Still, this argument is not sufficient to support a continued reliance on a 19th-century method for finding library materials.

On the other hand, nearly every major academic library has one administrator who is on the "cutting edge" of everything electronic. This person is frequently the bane of a special collections librarian's existence. Many techno-administrators even encouraged the wholesale scanning of collections that otherwise would have required many hours of preservation processing (rehousing or even microfilming), with the ultimate goal of destruction of the originals to save space and money over the years. In many cases, that was the greatest fear expressed by many special collections librarians who thought that their collections were in jeopardy of destruction if they scanned a single page. Fortunately, techno-administrators and special collections librarians have reached a point of understanding regarding the lack of professional standards for the creation, storage, maintenance, and migration of electronic collections and the protection of the book as an artifact and information storage device.

Still, the techno-administrator urges the manuscript librarian to digitize collections, mark them up with EAD, HTML, and Dublin Core metadata. The humble manuscript librarian shakes her head, sighs, and points to the mountain of unprocessed collections as evidence that digitizing an already processed collection is a grand waste of time and money, and the battle lines are drawn.

To a certain point, the manuscript librarian is correct. As a compromise, many special collections librarians have opted to convert their collections' paper-finding aids to electronic format. At many libraries, these finding aids are part of a virtual library, digital library, or whatever the catch-phrase of the day is for this particular point of access. The majority of finding aids are electronically searchable and can be located utilizing one of the many available Web browsers. The electronic-finding aid is not revolutionary, it is simply a new way of delivering a traditional end-product of a processed collection. This is but one example of the many ways special collections librarians have been more progressive in their thinking about the potential for electronic access to their collections.

We have arrived in the 21st century. We are not a paperless, postindustrial society and special collections librarians still have jobs caring for paper-based collections. Each step forward on the path of electronic storage is carefully measured. National standards for the preservation and care of electronic information are still being debated. Biblio-Luddites point to 5 1/4" floppy disks and say, "See, I told you so. We don't have a single computer that can read what's on that disk." Nicholson Baker continues to chide librarians who are desperately trying to keep up with the effects of acid hydrolysis by microfilming materials before they are too brittle to open. More journals are published electronically every year and consumers still prefer a paper-based book to one they can read on a hand-held device.

Special collections librarians even hear the occasional administrator say, "Everything anyone needs is on the Internet." To which I reply, "Really? Show me your dissertation." For now, I can say it with relative confidence knowing that the administrator cannot comply with my request. But that day is coming. University archivists are among those leading the fight to abandon dissertations and theses on paper in favor of electronic versions maintained by companies outside of their libraries.

Microfilm, microfiche, CD-ROMs, books, databases, newspapers, and even microcards continue to peacefully cohabit libraries. No one medium has fully replaced another and it is highly unlikely that it will ever happen that way. Special collections librarians continue to adapt their traditional ways of providing information and caring for the book as an artifact and information storage device. They have to. For if one day all materials are published electronically, then all paper-based books will be rare.

45

Selling Instruction

Communicating the Value of the Library in the Age of the Internet

Michael J. Rose

I have heard advice given to students considering careers as academic librarians that goes something like this: learn as much as you can about computers and technology. From my perspective, this particular bit of advice seems to miss the point of what a librarian does. Yes, technology skills are necessary, but does this advice really mean anything? Consider the analogy of a young aspiring car salesman being advised that he should learn as much as he can about driving. While the ability to drive may be essential to the car salesman, it won't help him with that part of his career that involves sales. Similarly, computer literacy is essential to a librarian, but it is merely a tool useful in accomplishing the goal of teaching research skills. Technology skills need to be addressed but not in the central way the opening sentence of this essay suggests. I will start with technology not because it is of primary importance but rather just to get it out of the way.

The only constant is change: this cliché aptly describes the discipline of librarianship at the present time. Certainly, the current environment demands that librarians be well-versed in computer skills. It is part of our daily lives in this profession to prepare for and adjust to the new version of a database. New computers with new operating systems are installed in public areas, and new or upgraded software often requires training. And the World Wide Web allows for much more than just text and hyperlinks. These new features need to be understood not just to assist patrons with their browsing, but also to possibly expand library services. That said, I would expect the response to these statements to begin with "So what?" This is the equivalent to the car salesman's ability to drive.

More important than this is the ability to tell the difference between new technology and necessary technology. Which things really improve services and which things merely make you look current? Even some self-styled technologists refer to the "cutting edge" as the "bleeding edge," suggesting that embracing the newest technology is not always the best course of action. But there is no way to simply know the difference. The ability to carefully consider new technology in the light of the core values of a particular academic library is essential. In most academic libraries there is a finite budget and a limited number of faculty and staff hours. Embracing a new technology has an opportunity cost which needs to be viewed in light of existing services. There are two pitfalls to be avoided: the desire to add an impressive new technology without consideration of the opportunity cost, and the reluctance to embrace a promising new technology because of a substantial staff-side learning curve.

Aside from the flux of new technology, the teaching role of an academic librarian should remain constant. The ability to teach effectively is the most important attribute of an academic librarian. I would argue that without the librarian imparting information literacy skills in an effective way, the value of any technology is seriously limited. It is unfortunate that students conducting research are often willing to settle for "good enough," and this approach is exacerbated by databases and search engines that allow students to gather more information with less focus. Unless, that is, a librarian has the opportunity to guide a student and introduce the various skills necessary for focused research and careful evaluation of the materials collected.

This is a time-consuming process requiring patience on the part of both librarian and student. Understanding the importance of information literacy goes without saying for an academic librarian, but the ability to convey the importance of this to a student is an important skill. Effectively imparting this concept to students may not merely improve their academic performance specifically, but may also improve their information-seeking behavior in general. As an example, I look back on the news coverage of recent elections where potential voters were asked about the candidates. One common answer I have noticed is "The candidate hasn't told us enough about himself for us to make a decision." I have always found this response troubling, as it implies a misunderstanding about the function of advertising in general, and campaign advertising in particular.

Advertising is not about educating; it is about shaping opinions and modifying behavior. More information is necessary, and on the surface it appears that the growth of technologies such as the World Wide Web should make preliminary research into candidates somewhat easier. But it hasn't. A surfeit of information isn't enough; more skills are needed to evaluate the information, to separate the wheat from the chaff. This is where the librarian's skills transcend the limits of technology. What is bias, reliability, et cetera? How can one find reliable information? There is a value to a librarian's ability to teach this that goes beyond making better students to making better citizens as well.

Unfortunately, all of this may be of little value without another skill: the ability to convey to teaching faculty and university administrations the importance of the services librarians offer. Libraries are expensive and, it appears, underused. Lack of use does not indicate lack of value as much as shifting expectations. Students find that it is time consuming to search a citation database and retrieve the item cited while Internet search engines are fast and easy to use. If students don't see the advantage in visiting the library and speaking to a librarian, then teaching faculty should be made aware of the advantage.

Librarians who can develop these interactions with teaching faculty and can begin to incorporate information literacy skills in the classroom will reinforce the importance of the library. If university administrations view the library in terms of a cost-benefit analysis and if usage is slipping, this interaction is essential. The administration must see the library as vital if they are to fund it, and teaching faculty must see it as essential if they are going to require its use by students. I have had the experience of speaking with teaching faculty about services and resources offered by my library only to discover that they had no idea such services and resources existed. Teaching faculty will be more likely to require library use when they understand what academic librarians do and what the library has to offer them. Students who are required to use the library may be inclined to use it again once they have benefited from it.

Librarians need to be comfortable with new technology but not consumed by it; focus on technology should never supersede the importance of instruction. As teaching is central, relationships with faculty across campus need to be fostered to make teaching information literacy possible. Academic librarians cannot withdraw to the comfort of their libraries but must be out selling themselves and their services to the campus. New technology in the library, in a sense, can be compared to those fancy new options a car dealer may use to lure you toward a purchase. But these options are worthless if the car does not run. In a similar fashion, new technologies may be the hook that draws patrons to the library, but the research and information literacy skills imparted by academic librarians are what make the time spent there worthwhile. Unless new librarians are willing to step out and sell themselves, their role as teachers will not be fully realized.

46

Militant Segregationists, Control Freaks, and Techno-Believers

Craighton Hippenhammer

Librarians of the new century will have a very different look: they will be militant segregationists, control freaks, and techno-believers. If these three core ideals do not happen, libraries will fade away, becoming empty hulks of their former selves, virtually replaced by commercial solutions and private-sector values.

Librarians have long been divided into two camps: public services and technical services. For a long time, this segregation has been seen as good—seen as a key element in the way librarians are trained and in the way their jobs are defined. In recent years, unfortunately, this distinction has been declining. It's time to reinvigorate the "separate camps" concept. Let's call them something new, too, like "content services" and "process services."

The last thing I wanted to be when I graduated from library school was a technical services librarian. I hated cataloging, thought acquisition duties should be relegated to clerks, and never even saw a computer during my MLS days. The first substantial part of my career, then, I spent in public services as a children's librarian in public libraries and as a reference librarian in an academic library. On the side, I kept up an interest in personal computers from their inception in the early 1980s. The expertise I gained from that hobby paid off in effecting technological change in more than one library, and I found that process both fascinating and challenging.

I think many if not most librarians prefer to be in one camp or the other, whether by interest, expertise, or personality type. Currently, I supervise Circulation, oversee Interlibrary Loan, run Information Technology, do my stint on the Reference Desk, help out with bibliographic instruction, and teach our two-credit library class. Am I feeling schizophrenic, torn, split apart? You bet. You know that feeling like you're attempting too much and not doing any of the things terribly well? Far too many of us are doing exactly that.

In academic libraries it has become very common for all librarians to be dragged out of their offices to cover the reference desk. Over the years, public services has gained power and technical services has lost prestige. Which services have come to be seen as important? Anything that has contact with patrons: readers' advisory; reference; instruction; storytelling. Libraries can't exist without catalogers and processors of books, but they can exist without reference librarians, et al.

Ah, but our library mission statement reads that we have a service orientation here at our library, you say. Since when is service limited to face-to-face contact? Do you always meet the mechanic that fixes your car? Or the radiologist that reads your CAT scan? And what is your reference librarian saying about her declining statistics because online research tools are replacing so many face-to-face "beautiful reference moments"?

The 21st-century librarian needs to come to realize that it is okay for many librarians not to be "content" (emphasis on first syllable) librarians. It's okay to be librarians involved only in the process of making information available and not in the memorization of content types, the location of information, or the knowledge of a literature. It's okay to be librarians involved only in the creation and processing of a physical or virtual library.

Never did I think I would ever support an argument in favor of catalogers (who now should all be called metadata librarians), but as an Information Technology Librarian, I believe we in process services must be freed to do what our job demands without always being pulled away constantly for this content service and that content service. Now that so many research and educational services can happen with no actual, face-to-face library visit, process services has already regained some of its power and influence. Library directors only have to recognize that fact so they can stop wasting valuable personnel resources. They simply have to be bold and say, "We will no longer do that face-to-face service so we can support that other growing, but more hidden, process service."

Let's be militant about segregating these two very different types of library work. It will concentrate talents and expertise and will help our virtual libraries to be a stronger presence in the world.

Librarians in the 21st century must also control their physical and virtual environments. Library schools should not train students who have little likelihood of becoming leaders. Controlling one's own work sphere can be as simple as creating a new and better way to do some task. Professionals create policies and procedures. Clerks and library assistants follow them. As elementary as this is, it is amazing how many librarians in charge insist on operating at a clerk level, by either keeping things always the same or by allowing others to make changes in their sphere of influence for them. Professional librarians must always be trying to improve the work processes around them. If they don't, libraries will gradually become irrelevant.

Librarians must also gain control over their virtual environments. Amazingly, this has been the most challenging for academic libraries. The difficulties are legion: institution home pages that have no direct link to the library; public relations departments that have been turning university Web pages into slick color-magazine marketing tools, and that insist the academic pages follow suit; computer centers that answer to the vice president of administrative services rather than the academic dean, and therefore serve professors and librarians after departments like admissions and alumni; computer centers that have a "turf" mentality, making it difficult to grow a library information technology department; the impossibility of adding information technology library staff to manage the new virtual presence, crucial especially in the big technical jump from static Web pages to interactive Web pages.

Gaining control over one's own virtual library presence challenges all types of libraries. Just being able to hire one's own technology talent has long been a problem, although with the recent collapse of the dot-coms, nonprofits have been recently hiring well-trained talent from the private sector. This window of opportunity is not likely to last long, however, as the more usual career path is to get experience and training in nonprofits and then move on to the higher salaries of the corporate world. Hiring librarians with technology expertise can also be a challenge. Having a librarian on staff to manage technology changes, upgrades, and applications has been crucial for libraries since the mid-1990s—someone who can see the big picture, recognize practical applications of important technologies to library situations, and be able to implement solutions that work.

Technology has been stripping control away from librarians now for more than a decade, and is the main reason why librarians must become control freaks. Control over selection decisions has suffered perhaps the severest blow. E-books and e-journals come in preselected packages, as do online indexes. The full-text of journals in online periodical databases come and go with no librarian input. To fight the high cost of these online products, libraries have to band together in consortia to gain leverage in cost negotiations. What is lost is local selection of databases and other online products that are tailored to a specific institution or community. Some consortia allow selective adoption of products negotiated for, but others do not.

Control is also seeping away from librarians in the areas of research technique (keyword vs. subject searching), fair use (software EULAs), and free speech (federal laws limiting Internet access in schools and libraries), and so on. Librarians must fight for control over their work policies and professional environment harder than ever, because if we don't control the technology, the technology will control us.

Librarians of the future must be believers in technology. It's no longer enough for non-IT librarians to send polite nods and faint compliments in its direction; they must be truly convinced that technology is necessary for their future survival. This convincing must be done in library school, where they should be trained in the basics—specifically in the ways technologies are applied to library situations. While not all librarians need to learn the ins and outs of implementing technologies, they need to be eager to work with technologies and capable of seeing where they can be applied to their work situations. Information technology librarians can suggest technology applications, but non-IT librarians need to be able to ask for technology solutions when work situations can be improved by them.

The personal computer has proved to be a revolutionary force in the workplace, increasing efficiency and speeding up laborious tasks. Fonts, graphics, manipulatable spreadsheets and databases, and word processing are all available on the desktop. The connected computer is having an even heavier impact on the way librarians do business, from providing patrons access to research materials to greatly increasing communication between library planning centers, between peers located at great distances, and even between librarians and students located in different states. Learning is increasingly done at home, and providing reading material over distances needs to be as convenient as ordering a book online from Amazon.com or groceries from a nearby Internet-connected food store. If librarians fail to provide both convenience and speed in the services they provide, private businesses will step up and fill the vacuum. Libraries need to continue being full-service nonprofit entities, and technology is a big part of that picture.

It is simply time to end the production of new librarians who want nothing to do with technology. We have enough dinosaurs out here now, and we don't need to be adding to them. We do need techno-believers who want to be able to control and improve the library services within their spheres of influence and are willing to fight for dropping nonessentials so they can concentrate their efforts on doing what they should be doing and doing it well.

47

Metaphor Matters
Imagining the Future of
Librarianship and the Library

Nancy Kuhl

About midway through the last course I took in library school, a class period was devoted to a discussion of new and possible future information technologies. A guest lecturer, a renowned faculty member in the university's communications department, talked about the latest developments in various technologies, and he hypothesized about the future of electronic communications and information. Throughout the discussion he continually made metaphoric connections between information technologies and the physical world, referring often to the "information environment," and the "future landscape" of communication and information technologies. Toward the end of the period, the energetic and engaging professor shook his head and said, "I hate to say it, but I think you are all entering a dying profession. Who is reading books in the library? The building is empty. How can you compete?" The professor's use of metaphors of physical space to describe digital and electronic information while at the same time reducing the actual physical library to an "empty building" seemed to imply a perceived conflict between the virtual world of information and the physical world of the library. The professor's metaphoric descriptions left a significant impression on me, and it occurred to me that the metaphors we chose to describe libraries and librarians might play a role in determining their futures.

The professor's rhetorical questions about the library's ability to compete with new technologies, of course, sparked a barrage of responses from students, none of whom were willing to concede that the end of the library—and librarianship—as we know it might be drawing near. The professor handily dismissed arguments about the need for many library services, the unlikelihood that whole library collections would ever be available digitally, the role libraries play as campus and community centers, the value of human contact and face-to-face interactions with librarians. "You know," the guest lecturer said as he gathered his things to leave the room, "in twenty or thirty years, I think the main library on campus will have been converted into a freshman dorm." And with that, he was gone, leaving us to contemplate an image of one possible future for the library.

It is this kind of idea—especially when it comes from a well-published scholar who feels that his research can all be done from his desktop or his Palm Pilot—that drives much of the current discussion and debate about libraries and librarianship. In the past few months alone, *American Libraries* ran a cover story entitled "The Last Librarian: A Cautionary Tale," and *The Chronicle of Higher Education* published a front page article and hosted an online colloquium both with the title "The Deserted Library." These sensational titles and articles certainly capture the imaginations of readers, pushing them to develop new ideas of libraries and future information technologies, and to generate new metaphors for how they might fit into research, scholarship, and the acquisition of knowledge. These imaginings, many of which predict the end of librarianship, are generally not entirely clear; they feel, somehow incomplete. This is due in large part to the fact that as yet we have been unable to imagine satisfactory new metaphors for libraries and librarians.

Metaphor—the human effort to expand language's reach by making comparisons between ideas, objects, and concepts—allows us to know and understand things because of their relationships to other things. When it comes to the library, the metaphors that have been used to describe the concept and its workings have been plentiful and they are instructive. Libraries, for instance, have been called the mind of a culture, or its immense memory. These metaphors reflect a perceived vastness of the information universe contained in libraries. And the term "universe," too, has often been used as a metaphor for the library—Jorge Luis Borges, in fact, begins his important story "The Library of Babel" thus: "The universe (which others call the library . . .")." In this metaphor, librarians are guides through the specific world of the library, tour guides leading others through a complex environment. The associative leaps made in describing libraries and librarians help us to understand the role libraries have played in human culture, and the roles they might yet play in an evolving "information landscape."

It is, perhaps, logical that many new technologies central to information storage and retrieval are described using the same metaphors that have in the past been associated with collections of books alone. The description of an electronic "environment" is conceptually so similar to that of the library as an information "universe" that they are arguably the same idea. The similarity in how we conceptualize new and old information media doesn't stop there. Computers are equipped with memories, and the Internet, some claim, puts the universe at one's fingertips. At a recent library conference I was given a button bearing the phrase: "Ask me! A librarian is a human search engine."

Our cultural imagination belies the human tendency to link like with like—one collection of information is basically like another, one method of seeking information is the same as the next. Such collapsing of the physical—books, human librarians, library buildings—with digital and electronic formats, mechanized search tools, and digital "environments" indicates the ease with which we have conceived of a future library that gathers, organizes, maintains and facilitates the searching of a collection of information including both old and new formats as well as formats we have not yet imagined.

In our choice of metaphors it seems clear that in our imaginations there is no necessary disconnect between the virtual and physical libraries. Though researchers and students may envision a complete virtual library including all the research tools they need and making them available to a personal computer, this idea hasn't yet filtered into our common language and our shared imagination. In the same way that the "paperless office" exists as an idea alongside the actual working office which is terrifically dependent on paper, the "virtual library" exists beside (or perhaps *inside*) the physical library. In the metaphors embedded in our language—the "folders" one keeps on a computer "desktop," the electronic "books" and "journals" in the virtual library—we can see that our current circumstances dictate the way we imagine the future; as yet, we have not imagined a new library that is significantly different from the model that exists in buildings the world over and, of course, on the Internet where directories like Yahoo.com use a library model to organize websites into categories that facilitate searching. Though libraries are certainly changing and librarians are taking on increasingly diverse kinds of work, appropriate new metaphors haven't yet surfaced to describe them.

This is not to say, of course, that new metaphors haven't influenced our cultural understanding of libraries and librarians. For example, the comparison of libraries and bookstores, a connection fueled by the addition of coffee shops and comfortable chairs to some campus libraries, is a popular and significant new metaphor. As a result of the idea that libraries might benefit from cultivating a likeness to bookstores, there is an increasing tension between the library and the market economy, and many librarians are struggling to determine whether or how libraries might emulate large bookstore chains, beyond simply serving coffee. There is no question that the adoption of market values would have a range of consequences in libraries, and these consequences are the subject of many debates in library literature. These debates are instructive in many ways, not the least of which is the fact that they highlight the power that the metaphors we choose have to shape our institutions and their futures.

If one doubts the strength of such a metaphoric connection, one need only notice the addition of links to Amazon.com in some online library catalog book records or the arrangement of some public library collections into new categorical groups, such as "Travel" and "Health," which ultimately render the materials' classifications and call numbers meaningless. And if one extends this metaphor to consider its consequences at library reference desks, if one attempts to negotiate the territory between librarians and retail salespeople, it becomes clear that any attempt to model reference service on sales is entirely inappropriate (which isn't to say that it isn't happening in some libraries). Though public service librarians must, as any salesperson, deal graciously and fairly with a diverse public, the business of answering reference questions and educating and assisting patrons is one where many market principles simply do not apply. The library customer, for instance, isn't and cannot always be right and the needs which bring one to the library are quite often more complex and more apt to need consultation, trial and error, and in-depth assistance than those that bring one to the supermarket. The market economy isn't a particularly apt metaphor for the library because the library doesn't fit into the "do or die" model of many industries. As a result, attempting to employ a retail model in libraries destines libraries to failure.

Libraries require a more flexible model, one that foregrounds the fluid nature of information technologies and libraries' ability to incorporate these new technologies into their complement of tools and resources and to use them to aid in meeting the needs of students and researchers. The common metaphor for librarians, that of guide through a landscape or leader through an information universe, seems appropriate to the work librarians do in assisting students with new and frequently changing information resources. The complexity of the current world of information is such that all but the most savvy and the most determined researchers are likely to find the research process to be excruciatingly difficult and rarely successful, especially if they have no access to assistance. The tour guide metaphor, then, while representing only a small fraction of the work librarians do, is useful in describing work with students, regardless of whether that work takes place in physical bookstacks or the digital paths of an electronic database.

The truth is that the best and most apt metaphors used to describe libraries and librarians are the old ones, the ones that have been used for ages. Librarians are, perhaps more than ever before, necessary guides, leaders, allies, escorts. And the library *is* the active mind of a culture, a metaphor that highlights the library's vastness, its illimitability. The library works to order a culture's knowledge in the way one's mind orders ideas, controls a chaos of language and image and impulse. Metaphors that tie the library to landscape or imagine it as its own world or universe, too, accurately describe the diverse and growing variety of information and formats collected; the research process does resemble a physical journey, through various terrains (some rewarding, some treacherous).

Though they are useful in many ways and do help us to stretch our understanding, metaphors are, in the end, incomplete representations. There is no final comparison that can replace the thing itself. Thus, even the most apt metaphors cannot fully represent the library's complex collection of ideas, thoughts, perceptions, perceptions of perceptions, expressions, representations, mistaken hypotheses. There can be little doubt that libraries are more than storage space for books and quiet study areas for students. The physical buildings, many of which are physically imposing structures designed to be monuments to knowledge and learning, are essential to our understanding of the library; however, they are only part of the story. Books, too, are only part of it. It is the indescribably vast body of—"information" is perhaps the only word, though it must be made to include much that would never be referred to as information—that the library contains both physically and ideologically that dictates our understanding of the concept "library."

Metaphors, too, serve to limit one's perceptions. If we say that information technology is a kind of landscape, we will think of it, approach it, and understand it in particular ways that are determined by our knowledge of and feelings about the concept "landscape." Popular misunderstandings about the work librarians do results in part from the metaphors by which our culture understands such work. Librarians are, in fact, guides of a sort, but they are also instructors, scholars, analysts, and thinkers. And we might build additional metaphors around the librarian's work by referring to her or him as a designer, an information architect, a treasure hunter, a collection builder. None of these, however, is likely to accurately or completely describe the day-to-day work of a librarian.

So it is inadequate, but metaphor is nevertheless an enormous part of developing perceptions and cultivating understanding. For this reason, it is crucial that librarians take control of the metaphors commonly used to describe both the work librarians do and libraries themselves. The more we dabble in inappropriate metaphors about our institutions—by trying to make them look like bookstores, for instance—the further we move the cultural understanding away from what libraries actually are and what they do and have been doing since their beginnings, namely collecting, preserving, ordering, and providing access to all manner of information. This, regardless of physical buildings, and paper books, and digital formats that need no actual space on the library's shelves. We must remind, first ourselves, then our patrons, that (virtual and physical) libraries are sites of transaction where silence and language meet, where the known and the unknown come together, where, intellectually speaking, anything can happen.

Books and buildings and human librarians will play a significant role in this, but it will be, foremost, a fluid role, one that will often be ambiguous and challenging. As a culture, we have been unable to imagine a satisfactory new metaphor for the library because though much has changed and will continue to change about the way libraries look and feel, they still fit into our culture in much the same ways they always have. And it is difficult to develop a new way of thinking about librarianship because for the time being librarians are often involved in the same kinds of work that they have always done, though perhaps they now do that work in new ways or with new tools (searching a paper index is like searching an online index is like searching . . .). That libraries and librarianship have evolved to accommodate new technologies, different sorts of patrons, increasingly diverse information needs is evidence that they can evolve still further to meet as yet unforeseen needs, to handle as yet unimaginable technologies and information formats. Of course, it is the work of librarians (Frontiersmen and women? Explorers? Navigators? Futurists?) to make the necessary changes happen, to keep ahead of the technology and changing information needs, to innovate, to anticipate what might come next and to be prepared for it. Librarians will define the new mind of the culture, the new information landscape. Librarians entering the field today and in the future must be able to face ambiguity and they must be willing to negotiate the old metaphors of the library and the new, because for at least the time being we will have to do both.

In October 1998, *American Libraries* ran a cover story called "Looking Ahead: 20 in their 20s" which included twenty young librarians' responses to questions about their ideas of librarianship, their careers, and the future of the library. The very first sentence of the article begins "With 40 or more working years ahead of them . . ."; with that in mind, it is no surprise that every respondent believed that libraries would thrive in the 21st century and beyond. Though they might change to accommodate new formats and technological trends, the young librarians claimed, libraries would continue much as they had for years before, as community and campus centers and guardians of cultural knowledge. With at least forty working years ahead of them, of course the librarians thought (hoped?) their chosen profession would not become obsolete in the near future.

Five of the librarians interviewed for "Looking Ahead" were born the same year I was. And though I join my peers and colleagues in the conviction that libraries can and will survive, evolve, flourish, and succeed in the years to come, librarians must be willing to transform libraries to meet the diverse and changing needs of complex communities of library users. To do this we must cultivate possibility. The future of libraries is uncertain and without the vision and effort of librarians, libraries may in fact disappear. Actually, if librarians refuse the current challenge—which is not to create new models for libraries, new metaphors for their functions in our culture, but to renew the profession's commitment to traditional library ideals while actively incorporating new technologies, different modes of research, developing media, and the diverse services users need to make use of these—it seems likely that libraries, and librarians, will slowly become obsolete.

The library is a culture's discontinuous articulation of itself; it is the keeper of the culture's ideas and secrets, its wishes, its nightmares and dreams, its failures, and its past as well as its imagination of its own future. In this way, it is a kind of world, a collage or a miniature representing the world it exists within. But the world and universe metaphors used to describe the library and developing information technologies are too vast and imprecise to give one a clear image which might aid in understanding the ways they might fit together into a unified whole including information in all its formats. At the same time, such metaphors imply too limited a role for librarians, both in the paper-only libraries of the past and in the multimedia libraries of the present and future. A better metaphor for the changing library is one the philosopher Ludwig Wittgenstein uses to describe language: "Our Language can be seen as an ancient city: a maze of little streets and squares, of old and new houses, and of houses with additions from various periods; and this surrounded by a multitude of new boroughs with straight regular streets and uniform houses."

Applying such a metaphor to the library asserts the interconnectedness of the library's traditional collections and the new formats it must strive to anticipate and incorporate. The ancient city metaphor reminds us that the library is vast but also growing, new and old at once, building and developing on its own foundations, creating and supporting scholarly beginnings as well as established paths of study. In such a metaphor, the representation of the librarian can be expanded to be more inclusive; here, the librarians might be the traditional guide, but he or she might also be builder, planner, citizen. As we try to maintain the strengths of the traditional metaphors but to eliminate some of their limitations, librarians might begin to reimagine the library and their role in it. They may, too, begin to re-envision the roles libraries play in their communities and in the lives of their patrons. What they imagine might be a rich new future for the library and for librarianship, one that is ripe with possibilities. Perhaps they discover a future in which the fear of the library's disappearance is just a small piece of the culture's boundless memory.

REFERENCES

Borges, Jorge Luis. "The Library of Babel," *Collected Fictions*, trans. Andrew Hurley (New York: Viking, 1998).

Carlson, Scott. "The Deserted Library," *The Chronicle of Higher Education* 48, no. 12 (2001): 35.

"Looking Ahead: 20 in their 20s," *American Libraries* 29, no. 9 (1998): 38.

Stevens, Norman. "The Last Librarian: A Cautionary Tale," *American Libraries* 32, no. 9 (2001): 60.

Wittgenstein, Ludwig. *Philosophical Investigations*, trans. G.E.M. Anscombe, 3rd ed. (Englewood: Prentice-Hall, 1999).

48

Seeking

Enthusiastic Artists

Randall M. MacDonald and Andrew L. Pearson

While the landscape of librarianship continues to change with the rapid development of technology, the experience of conducting seven job searches over a four-year period suggests that the most desired characteristic for tomorrow's librarians has roots in a traditional concept, the view of librarianship as an art.

Roux Library serves the community of Florida Southern College, a four-year, private, coeducational institution with a strong liberal arts emphasis. More than forty undergraduate majors are offered to the 1,750 full-time students. The library also supports a master of business administration program and a satellite program in Orlando. Roux Library has a collection of more than 170,000 book volumes, 725 periodical subscriptions, and more than 5,000 audiovisual items—audio CDs, videotapes, and DVDs.

The library conducted seven job searches in four years in both public services and technical services. Included were two unsuccessful searches for the position of Reference/Interlibrary Loan Librarian, two successful searches and one unsuccessful search for the position of Access Services Librarian, one successful search for the position of Resource Sharing Librarian, and one successful search for the position of Catalog Librarian.

These positions are part of a team of six librarians, 3.75 FTE paraprofessionals, and 3.95 FTE student assistants during the academic year.

The search committee in each instance included three or more librarians and at least one faculty representative from an academic department. The interview process included an opportunity to meet with other faculty members; in the preliminary search for a Reference/Interlibrary Loan Librarian, presentation of a professional portfolio and a simulated classroom instructional session were required.

The positions were identical in that they were entry-level positions. Qualifications varied primarily in regard to skills associated with the position, e.g., detailed familiarity with the OCLC ILL subsystem for the Resource Sharing Librarian position. The number of applicants varied considerably between the first search (1996) and searches completed in 1998 and 2000. The unsuccessful job search for the Reference/Interlibrary Loan Librarian attracted more than 120 applicants. More recent job searches received as few as four and as many as fifteen applications.

GAUGING POTENTIAL FOR SUCCESS

The characteristics shared by successful librarians at Florida Southern mirror those of librarians at most institutions, and may be classified as skill characteristics and personal characteristics. Skill characteristics include expertise in at least one sphere of librarianship, the ability to communicate clearly, a talent for teaching, and essential computer skills, including knowledge of electronic database searching and Web page creation. Further, applicants are usually expected to have pursued an academic and professional career path that reflects an interest in college librarianship. Personal characteristics include a pleasant disposition, flexibility and creativeness in thought and action, an interest in learning and professional development, self-motivation, and an enthusiastic, cooperative spirit. A sense of humor is a welcome bonus.

A more desired, but elusive, quality emerged from further evaluation of these searches that included the ability to synthesize and practically apply both sets of characteristics to a fluid library environment. We termed this quality "the art of librarianship."

This quality draws a contrasting relationship between two essential elements of librarianship—librarianship as a science and as an art. Librarianship as a science reflects the characteristics of a traditional scientific discipline. Its focus centers on the use of scientific methodology to study and interpret aspects of library services and collections, including the observation of behaviors or processes, the gathering of quantitative data, and developing conclusions that generate formulae, rules, or principles that serve to interpret observations.

In contrast, the art of librarianship in its most basic form may be simply defined as the practical application of library science. However, the precise nature of this definition detracts from the nuance in the word "art" that defies exactness. In extending the previous definition for the art of librarianship, our review of desirable characteristics in librarians intends to describe the art of librarianship as the craft of uniting the elements of library science; that is, a systematic approach of skills, facts and principles, with a librarian's personal abilities and effectively applying this within the interpersonal, environmental dynamics of one's library. How would a candidate interact with the library staff, students, other faculty, and within our unique community? How effectively would a candidate impart a sense of understanding the way information is organized and used to library patrons?

In practice, our search process for these seven searches included, formally or informally, an evaluation of a librarian's command of both the science and art of librarianship. Initial evaluation of a candidate began with his or her knowledge of the science of librarianship. For our search process, once this had been met, the process quickly progressed to the art of librarianship. The level of "artistic ability" as represented in the résumé and discussions with Endnotes, and demonstrated in the telephone and on-site interviews was assessed and influenced the committee's decision for future employment.

In the case of recent searches at Florida Southern, one aspirant applied for each of three concurrently available positions. The candidate exhibited the technical skills that initially suggested suitable placement for any of the positions, even though the positions were in divergent areas. As the search progressed through a stringent evaluative process, the committee unanimously agreed that the candidate and library would best be served if the candidate was offered the position of Access Services Librarian; the candidate showed greatest promise toward mastering the art of librarianship as it relates to that realm of our profession. Our search process was validated by her successful service to the library.

IF IT WERE AS EASY AS FISHIN' YOU COULD BE A MUSICIAN

With apologies to Bachman-Turner Overdrive, if it were as easy as dispassionately observing behaviors, gathering data, and developing rules, one would not necessarily be a successful librarian. Teaching and modeling the artistic side of librarianship as a complement to the science-like or rules-based foundation of librarianship is a challenge for library and information science schools. Some practitioners gravitated to librarianship specifically because they are comfortable with precisely defined rules of operation, and library schools have evolved from traditional foci to attract students in various information-centered fields only tangentially related to traditional librarianship.

It has served librarians well to use scientific characteristics as a framework for professional activity, but artistic ability allows one to synthesize hard data for application in fluid settings. The science of librarianship has a tendency to overshadow the art of what we do, but the art provides our means for flourishing in a service-oriented, people-filled environment. This was as true thirty, as twenty, as ten years ago, and will continue to be the case.

49

Before We Look to the Future . . .

Liz Kocevar-Weidinger

Enoch Pratt called the library a place "where races, ages, and socioeconomic classes mingled and people could educate themselves."[1] More recently, Michael Gorman stated that libraries are about the preservation, dissemination, and use of recorded knowledge so that humankind may become more knowledgeable and through knowledge reach understanding; and, as an ultimate goal, achieve wisdom.[2] Now, how do we rearticulate these visionary statements for the 21st century? I contend that problems regarding the structure of our intellectual discipline, changing technology, and economic factors must be resolved before we can forecast the future of librarianship.

INTELLECTUAL DISCIPLINE

For our profession to shape its future paradigm, we must decide who is responsible for that determination. I believe the fracture between the educators and the profession creates a void in leadership and decision making that results in others determining our future. Librarians who earn a terminal MLS degree gain a practical and theoretical foundation of knowledge. But how terminal is an MLS degree since our discipline produces a Ph.D. as well? Ph.D. scholars study information theory and institutions that administrate information, while the MLS librarian has a practical working knowledge of individual libraries. Dewey insisted that librarianship was a "mechanical art" in which emphasis was placed on practical matters.[3] Did Dewey's pragmatic, mechanical theory turn the MLS into little old ladies who wear cardigans and tell people to be quiet? Do those with a Ph.D. in Library Science consider those with an MLS to be their "colleagues" and vice versa? Although Ph.D.s have much to contribute to the theoretical framework of librarianship, the profession consists largely of those with an MLS. The profession needs to be more cohesive and MLS librarians need to be more assertive about their place in the future of librarianship.

TECHNOLOGY

Currently, rapidly evolving technologies drive much of the change in our discipline. I do not suggest that we change our philosophy or shift paradigms as quickly or as often as Yahoo changes its content, but I question our ability to proactively shape the future when we cannot foresee how the Internet and technology will impact us six months or ten years from now. Over time, theories and definitions championed by scholars such as Pratt and Gorman may hold true, but we must decide what our role will be in the application of service delivery in an environment that is impacted by rapidly changing technological innovations.

Part of that service delivery involves public search engines and directories and proprietary databases. Our attempts to stake our claim on the organization of information on the Internet in its infancy have failed, leaving us disenfranchised from the new world of knowledge. Instead, Yahoo, Google, and AltaVista have organized the Internet. Yes, most search engines or directories have staff with library degrees, but most Internet knowledge organizers do not. Do they do a better job? I do not know. We cannot foresee our future until we begin to participate more in shaping it via the Internet. While AltaVista and others continue to organize the public Internet, former librarians whose decisions are based on commercial profit rather than altruistic goals of preservation and dissemination of information are structuring our proprietary indexing and abstracting databases. The library profession's role in this relationship is passive; as user group members, we react to products that are flawed. This is inefficient and often nonproductive. Commercial providers need to be made aware that providing better service and being guided by user groups will lead to greater commercial viability and librarians must get more involved in creating and organizing this information sector. We need to decide what our role should be, if that role is attainable considering the commercial nature of public and proprietary search engines, and then pursue it aggressively if our profession is to be considered in the future service of information delivery via the Internet.

ECONOMICS

During the opening speech at the LOEX Convention 2001, Dr. Linda S. Dobb, executive vice president, Bowling Green State University, stated that the academic librarian's status is dependent on generating FTE income. Administrators want to see a tangible outcome for their investment. Before the Internet, statistics on acquisitions, circulation, and reference transactions were quantifiable items that we could use to justify our existence. However, listserv threads and IPED statistics demonstrate that these numbers are going down. Administrators may decide that new statistics such as Internet and database usage justify the acquisition of databases and a Web page designer, not a library.

Our discipline is not structured to charge for use nor evaluate the patron's attainment of knowledge. Enoch Pratt's statement that people can educate themselves in the library is true. However, do we provide a quality education, or even a successful leisure experience? When dividing tax dollars, would legislators prefer to give money to institutions that educate people and produce assessed outcomes, or to a library that provides an environment where learning is encouraged but not measured? Our discipline depends on administrators and legislators realizing the need for this intangible service. How can we determine our own future when we do not know what financial resources will be available? Once again, we are placed in a reactionary position. We may know what we would like to do, but how can we make strategic plans without reliable fiscal support? So we wait for our yearly budget to decide the future of that year. Does this mentality affect how our leaders (who are they again?) form long-term goals and paradigms? As long as we compete with other services that produce tangible outcomes and we rely on unstable funding, our future may be bleak.

CONCLUSION

To define our future we must have strong and well-rounded leadership without divisiveness and conflict over credentials. We must put forth and execute a visionary agenda as a reactive discipline that considers the outside forces of technology and economics, or have the agenda be that we move from being a reactionary to a proactive discipline. If we fail to establish an agenda and control that agenda, we will fail to define what constitutes a library and more importantly what is not a library, and allow others to define the term for us. I believe that until these issues are resolved, we cannot determine our future.

NOTES

1. Barbara Levin, "The Public Library as Great Equalizer," *American Libraries,* September 2000, 51.

2. Michael H. Harris, *History of Libraries in the Western World,* 4th ed. (Lanham, MD.: Scarecrow Press, c1995), 291.

3. Walt Crawford and Michael Gorman, *Future Libraries: Dreams, Madness, & Reality* (Chicago: American Library Association, 1995), 5.

50

Teaching Excellence and the Academic Librarian

Paralleling the Teaching Faculty's Track

Martha Henn McCormick

In the fall of 2001, a posting on the POD listserv, the e-mail discussion list for the Professional and Organizational Development Network in Higher Education, listed a count of approximately 300 centers for teaching excellence at institutions of higher learning in the United States. A quick check of the University of Kansas's Center for Teaching Excellence website that lists U.S. teaching centers [http://www.ku/edu/~cte/resources/websites/unitedstates.html] provides links, as of January 2002, to a total of 221 separate colleges and universities with teaching centers that have a Web presence, and many of these campuses list more than one office or center per campus. Additionally, the University of Kansas site lists more links for community colleges with teaching centers, and for professional organizations like the Professional and Organizational Development Network in Higher Education and the National Teaching and Learning Forum. Undeniably, as teaching faculty have been asked to do more with innovation in their pedagogy and the incorporation of technology into their teaching, many colleges and universities have beefed up support for faculty development in the areas of pedagogy and technology and many campuses have also put into place reward systems that recognize innovations and improvement in teaching and in the use of instructional technologies.

For teaching faculty, then, professional expectations regarding excellence in teaching and participation in the scholarship of teaching and learning have escalated greatly in recent years. As campuses move more aggressively into the realm of distance education and the offering of Web-based courses, the needs that their faculties have for help with pedagogical transformations and instructional technologies will only increase. For the academic librarians of the 21st century, our need to parallel our teaching faculty colleagues in how aggressively we take advantage of these opportunities to improve our pedagogy will be ratcheted up by several degrees, even in the near term. Gretchen Douglas argues, "In the future . . . the model of librarian as professor will be one of the many accepted roles of the profession."[1] Douglas, in her position, teaches credit-bearing courses related to computer applications; probably the majority of academic librarians who instruct are currently teaching library- and information-related instruction for existing courses rather than teaching credit-bearing courses, though others of us do teach full-term courses pertaining either to information retrieval and evaluation skills or in content areas for which we possess graduate degrees.

Teaching faculty have had to move away from the lone scholar mentality and open themselves up to more collaborative models of teaching. They routinely now participate in teaching workshops, in mentoring programs with designated master teachers on their campuses, in intensive and ongoing consultation relationships with teaching centers on their campuses, and so forth. As instruction moves ever more to the front and center of academic librarianship, librarians, too, must embrace these methods in order to become more relevant and better classroom instructors and to be understood within our campus cultures as instructional professionals in our own right. We must be part of the mix in the teaching workshops. We must be known as practitioners of pedagogical transformation and reform.

In 1987, Harold Shills described cutting-edge bibliographic instruction at that early moment of the electronic information age in these terms:

Bibliographic instruction has emerged to enjoy wide-spread, though not universal, acceptance in academic libraries. . . . Using learning theories and additional knowledge from education, psychology, and other disciplines, instruction librarians have developed sophisticated user-education programs. Advancing beyond an earlier emphasis on library orientation and individual research tools, these new approaches focus on concepts such as information structure and research strategy and use innovative learning approaches. . . . Course-related and course-integrated instruction has displaced the library tour as the preferred form of presentation.[2]

As Shills predicts, fifteen years later, our library instruction is no longer strictly bibliographic in nature but ranges over the information spectrum. Yet too often, while our content has shifted dramatically, we have not yet adopted these newer attitudes toward continuous improvement and assessment in instruction and are still the lone scholars. If teaching faculty do not encounter librarians as colleagues who are participating in pedagogical professional development opportunities, they are less likely to think of us as instructional peers and less likely to be open to, let alone seekers of, collaborative opportunities to work with academic librarians on meeting their students' information needs.

Deborah Grimes made a similar argument in 1993, six years after Shills' article, when she wrote,

[W]e must seek recognition by faculty and students that the library is indeed part of the instructional program. . . . One way that librarians can do this is by having the same commitment to instruction as other faculty. We can make sure that librarians are involved in college-wide curriculum development and in the design of new courses. We can make sure that our library instruction programs meet the same criteria as other classes, complete with written objectives, means of evaluation, and research. We can see that our library instruction programs receive budgetary attention, and, therefore, legitimacy within the overall educational process.[3]

Grimes argues that it is by such methods that we show teaching faculty that we librarians are knowledgeable in our own subject matter and that we are using the same instructional techniques that they use: "[L]ibrarians must cultivate a different relationship with teaching faculty, showing them that we are serious ourselves about the teaching role of the librarian and that we are serious educators."[4]

The operative word in Grimes' passage is "showing." We can tell faculty that we are serious about our teaching role but our participation in the scholarship of teaching and learning and in opportunities for our professional development as instructors demonstrates that commitment for them. In order for the participation of academic librarians in instructional professional development to be complete, it must be multi-pronged. Instead of endlessly discussing collaboration as a one-to-one equation between librarians and teaching faculty, we should approach collaboration in the instructional arena as teaching colleagues do: through the mediation and professional support mechanisms of the teaching centers on our campuses. If we meet our teaching colleagues in teaching workshops, and if we get hooked up with the teaching center professionals on our campus who can assist us in taking our instructional skills to new levels, then we plug into a powerful network on our campuses. We meet the faculty who are most interested in curricular reform and in taking advantage of informational and instructional technologies. It's an environment tailor-made for advancing the instructional programs and agendas of academic libraries.

The further we can carry these relationships between academic librarians and teaching centers, the better. Centers then begin to identify us librarians as the experts that we are in the area of information evaluation, research skills, and incorporating information effectively into the curriculum, and they bring us into the consultation process with faculty who are in the midst of redesigning their classes—a perfect time for librarians to assume an instructional role in those classes. There is no better way to be seen as an instructional professional in your own right than when a faculty member is steered to you by the very center on your campus designed to provide top-notch instructional assistance to faculty. In many cases, these centers are even housed in campus libraries; often such spatial proximity is not capitalized on.

Centers for teaching can also begin to understand the special pedagogical needs of librarians and can cater to them. We need workshops that help us plan highly effective lesson plans, since we often have only one or two class sessions with a given group of students. In many cases, we aren't building semester-long syllabi. Instead, we need to know how to be most effective in and capitalize on short-term instruction. We need to know how to identify our teaching philosophy so that we can know what we are about and where our strengths lie as instructors. We need to learn to build portfolios identifying our teaching successes when we don't have the luxury of end-of-semester course evaluations and struggle to gather in-depth assessments of student learning and evaluations of our students' long-term retention of what we teach. We need workshops that help us build community quickly in a classroom because we don't have fifteen weeks in which to build rapport with students; more often we have only fifteen minutes. Our opportunities as librarians to improve our instructional capabilities and document our professional development, thereby advancing our careers, can clearly be enhanced through such affiliations with teaching centers.

Centers for teaching and offices of professional development are experts in planning and delivering programming to faculty. Yet their staffs, like other academic professionals, are stretched thin. If academic librarians develop relationships with their campus teaching centers, often we can plan and offer workshops for faculty under the aegis of the teaching center. In the same way that we can deepen relationships to individual faculty members by being introduced to them through teaching centers, we can reach out to many members of the teaching faculty at a time through presenting programming. Centers have the event planning and promotional gears already in place and use resident faculty often to lead workshops on new instructional opportunities. Librarians should be leading some of these workshops. Not all academic libraries have a strong history of event planning and program development over time. To offer workshops on a spotty or piecemeal basis is often an exercise in frustration: promotion is difficult and our authority and credibility may have to be reestablished every time. If we can offer workshops for faculty through our teaching center, the umbrella of their professional credibility on campus covers us and we can take advantage of their promotional mechanisms already in place.

If we are looking for ways to incorporate information resources and library instruction into the curriculum on our campuses, then working with teaching centers is a tremendous new way to think of academic collaboration and can yield a bounty of positive results for the librarian of the new century. If we are looking for ways to solidly establish our instructional credibility and demonstrate our career commitment to pedagogical improvement, then we should turn to our teaching center staff and ask them to provide instructional training of a sort relevant to the type of teaching we as academic librarians most frequently do. If we want a venue for meeting faculty members who are likely to be open to information instruction in their classes, we can meet them in professional development workshops on your campus and through relationships brokered by teaching consultants on your campus. A rich relationship between an academic library and a center for teaching excellence is a forward-thinking approach to library instruction in the 21st century.

NOTES

1. Gretchen V. Douglas, "Professor Librarian: A Model of the Teaching Librarian of the Future," *Computers in Libraries* (Nov. 1999): 24–29. *Academic Search Elite.* EbscoHost. University Lib., IUPUI [cited 11 January 2002]. Available online at <http://www.ulib.iupui.edu>.

2. Harold B. Shills, "Bibliographic Instruction: Planning for the Electronic Environment," *College & Research Libraries* 48 (1987): 435–36.

3. Deborah J. Grimes, *The Library-Classroom Link: History, Theory, and Application,* ERIC ED 364 227 (1993): 20–21.

4. Grimes, 21–22.

51

The Library at the University of Vermont in 1900

Karl Bridges

This is a book about change. I thought it appropriate, then, since my contributors took on the task of looking forward, for me to put on my historian's hat and look into the past. By concluding with a look back we can, perhaps, have a better perspective on the road ahead.

I thought that it would be especially instructive for the readers to see a library report from the University of Vermont from 1900. Excerpts from this report, which conclude this essay, were made available through the courtesy of the Special Collections and Archives of the University of Vermont, and they provide an interesting look at an important period of library development. Aside from its strictly antiquarian interest, this report comes from an era of change for the university libraries as the university was undergoing a transformation from a small school, rooted in the traditional liberal arts, to a larger and more dynamic institution more focused on modern science. It also marks an important period as it was written during the tenure of the university's first professional librarian, who was also the first woman to head the library.

Throughout the 19th century the university had followed the traditional model of academic librarianship of the period—being opened for only brief periods each week and, when open, serving as a repository of books where students were not encouraged to linger. As one librarian's report stated in the 1860s, "The library has been open twice a week for the delivery of books. It was found impracticable to open it every day for consultation during the cold weather, by reason of the difficulty and expense of warming the hall. . . ." The librarian was normally a professor in some other subject who took on the additional library duties as an extra responsibility.

In 1900 the university libraries were led by its first woman librarian, Edith Emily Clarke, who prior to coming to Vermont had had a distinguished career as chief of cataloging at the Library of Public Documents in Washington, D.C., and, after her departure from Vermont in 1910, went on to a career as a library professor in California. It is unclear how the university arrived at its decision to hire Clarke, but statements made to the local newspaper at the time stated that "the library committee are confident that they have made a fortunate selection in their new professor of Books and Reading."

Despite these initial kind words the reality of the situation was that Edith Clarke had to deal with a library committee of male professors that was simply not going to hand over control of the library to her. This group, consisting of the university president and three professors, had had extensive experience with library affairs prior to her arrival and wasn't that interested in ceding authority to her.

In contrast to present library practice the librarian had very little autonomy in how the library was operated. Almost every decision, no matter how small, had to be considered and approved by the library committee. This isn't to say that the librarian had no influence, but the library committee did serve as oversight regarding almost every aspect of practical operational matters. One area where this was obvious was the issue of library staffing. The librarian reviewed applications and chose her employees, but these decisions were subject to the review (and sometimes the interference) of the library committee.

Library staffing was minimal. Prior to beginning of the 1899 school year Edith Clarke had no assistance in the library with the exception of the janitor, Henry Lord, who, she noted, "in the intervals of his duties as janitor assists very intelligently in the non-clerical branches of the library work." In October Clarke hired an assistant, Miss Mary R. Bates, who worked six hours daily. Evidently her work was quite satisfactory as Clarke states that "She has shown exceptional ability for the scholarly work of cataloguing and classifying, and she has been kept exclusively at that."

Student workers played an important role in the library—doing such work as retrieving items, reshelving books, and straightening up the library. In the 1898–99 term there had only been one student who worked twelve hours weekly. Clarke insisted that the student actually apply himself to library work, commenting that "he has been required to give all of these twelve hours to the desk, instead of studying his lessons between calls at the desk, as has been previously allowed." Thus illustrating that the question of whether to allow student library workers to study is an eternal one—probably incapable of resolution.

A good description of the circumstances surrounding work of student assistants was given by Clarke in reply to a letter of inquiry from a minister in New Hampshire seeking employment for his son who was entering the university: "In reply to your inquiry in regard to student work in this library for college expenses I will say at the outset that it is difficult for a freshman to obtain this work, although anyone is eligible after his first year. There is no difficulty in a young man of the right kind obtaining work to help him through college, and it becomes easier to find as the quality of his work becomes known. The library tasks are more confining and finicky than others. They require 12 hours a week, rated at 15 cents an hour the first year and 20 cents thereafter. This is only in credit in college bills not in cash."

Clarke reviewed applicants for positions with the president of the university. A letter of 1907 discussed the general issue of applicants for three open positions for student workers, commenting on the strengths and weaknesses of each. One student was an issue because she "did not have a very good record as a student" while another, while highly rated, was rejected because "it has been thought better not to give library places to freshmen so long as underclassmen of equal grade are available."

The comment by Clarke on one applicant is especially revealing: "Mr. Conrad A. Adams has been an applicant now for more than a year. I have heard so much that was good about him that I took pains to meet him when I was in Stowe this summer, and was very favorably impressed. I think he might be able to relieve me by writing my letters, and his familiarity with the typewriter would come into service in many ways." Technology skills, such as using a typewriter (as difficult for most people in 1900 as a computer is today) were seen as important, but, equally, so were personal impressions and scholarly characteristics which, in many cases, were the determining factors in the hiring decisions. In an era with limited financial resources and no system of student loans, library work, as these comments make clear, served to some extent as a scholarship device—somewhat in the same manner as our present-day system of college work study.

Student workers aside, the librarian also had to deal with applications for professional positions as they became available. One applicant in 1906, Eliza Clevenger, appeared highly qualified. Her background, as stated in her letter of application, included a library degree from Drexel Institute Library School and work experience, besides cataloging of a private library, at the library of Bryn Mawr College. Her responsibilities included "entire charge of the circulation department, of the periodical department, and of all books reserved for class use." In her References, aside from several from out of state, she included Miss Sarah C. Hagar, librarian of the Fletcher Free Library in Burlington and Miss Frances Hobart, secretary of the Free Public Library Commission in Cambridge, Vermont. This listing of local References, despite Clevenger's lack of local residence or employment, suggests, although the scope of this essay precludes a further examination, the existence of personal and professional networks existing between working professional women in early 20th-century Vermont.

The following are excerpts from the annual report of the librarian. I think it illustrates that, in general, librarians then as now had similar challenges and faced up to them well. Although the circumstances are distinctly different today, I think that any librarian reading this will see echoes of their own experience in issues of collection development, budget, instruction, and library planning. Now, with this brief preface, I will leave Edith to speak for herself.

TO THE PRESIDENT AND BOARD OF TRUSTEES OF THE UNIVERSITY OF VERMONT AND STATE AGRICULTURAL COLLEGE:

On the 31st of May 1899, the library of university contained 56,057 volumes, counting the Marsh Library of 12,507 volumes. During the past year there have been added 3,376 volumes, making a total of 59,433. These numbers include not only all bound volumes, counting the bound volumes of periodicals as come from the bindery, but also all paper covered books which are considered important enough to catalogue and to record in the accession book, from which these figures are taken. They do not include the Stevens-Whittingham gift, as it has not been possible as yet to record that, although the books are used when needed. . . .

There have been employed in the library during the year one cataloger working six hours a day; two students each working one and five-sevenths hours per day including Sunday; and a janitor who attends to the mail, prepares part of the binding, does pasting and mending of the books, and fills in odd hours at the loan desk, in addition to his care of the building and grounds. . . .

. . . At the beginning of the term the librarian gave the freshmen three lectures on the use of the library, the catalogue, and these reference books. The work was a made a required study and the exercises were given requiring use of the catalogue and these books. The notes given to the class were revised by the librarian and handed back with the hope that they would be of service to the student throughout his entire course. . . . This instruction as to how to make use of a library is by far the most important function of the modern university librarian, and is not supplied by any other part of the college curriculum. . . . The real use of reference books to a student is not in that one subject of which, according to the old maxim, he aims to know everything, but in those myriad other branches of knowledge of which the cultured man should always know something. . . . The library should be systematically arranged and catalogued before you turn a mob of young people into it . . . considering that students do not begin to use the library till their junior year, and do not use it very much until their senior year—whether more would not have been accomplished for the time and labor had the lectures been given as an elective to the juniors. It is not believed by the librarian that a series of popular talks with no exercises would be of the slightest benefit to the freshmen. Whether such talks would benefit a picked class of juniors would be subject for experiment. . . . An impediment to the library's affording the best service to the students arises from the building being planned without the full recognition of the work to be done in it. I allude to the provision of but one toilet room, the absence of a lobby where conversation could be carried on, and especially to the lack of special study or seminary rooms, where an instructor could meet his students with his books about him. . . .

Respectfully submitted,
Edith E. Clarke, Librarian
June 24, 1900

52

The Most Important Thing They Don't Tell You in Library School

Janet T. O'Keefe

There are many qualities that make up a good librarian, many of which are studied in library school. Professors will tell you at length why you must be committed to intellectual freedom and how you go about protecting it. They will teach you about diversity and give you exercises designed to test your commitment to being open and nonjudgmental. They will test you on the details of the profession, your ability to catalog a book or recommend valid sources or evaluate material for purchase. There is one skill, however, that you will need every day of your career and that your professors do not teach you: customer service.

Make no mistake—librarianship is a customer service profession. That is the essential thing to know if you want to continue and prosper in your work. Every day, you will be asked to deal with a wide range of people who have their own needs. You will have to be pleasant to them, even when your head pounds so badly that you think it will explode. You will have to help them with their problems when you feel buried by your own. And you must always exhibit an open and friendly manner to all comers.

You probably think this sounds horrible and that the job is impossible. That's because you have not yet learned the customer service skills that, when properly taught and practiced, will allow you to adopt a smooth, unruffled countenance in order to get through any type of encounter. These skills help you know that an upset customer probably has other issues on his or her mind that may mean a reaction on that particular day is temporary—and not that you, the librarian, are either a poor professional or, worse, a bad person. These skills help you see the entire context of your work and realize that negative encounters are not the sum of your work.

Customer service skills ensure that your patrons get better service in a happier environment. Good customer service rubs off on the patrons and the morale of the entire organization. In short, developing good customer service skills is the best thing you can do for yourself, your patron, and your library. Library science programs don't teach customer service skills. These programs don't teach you what to say to the patron who has lost an hour of work in the computer—after tech support has gone home for the day. Library professors rarely, if ever, discuss how to gracefully explain to the Wiccan standing by your reference desk that you have no books about her religion, not because you don't approve, but because the books are all stolen as quickly as you can purchase them.

Why don't library schools teach customer service? They may feel that such a technical skill isn't a graduate level function. They may feel that mentioning it is enough. It's likely that such programs have bought into the belief that customer service skills are born and not taught. The chances are that you will find no courses and, aside from a brief training seminar (maybe), you'll have to pick it up on the job.

People need to ask. If you want to improve your profession, start asking library science programs and library administrators to emphasize this skill more. Ask the hard questions. If you are an administrator, start demanding these skills in the people you hire and in the training programs you hire from. Insist that libraries have the same level of customer service that you expect from high-end retail stores or your local bank tellers. Maybe, if we ask, we will get the training that is required for the 21st century.

53

Technical Services Librarians for the 21st Century

What Are We Looking For?

Gwen M. Gregory

When you hear the phrase "technical services," what comes to mind? A librarian, holed up in the "back room," sorting through stacks of catalogs to order new additions for the collection? Someone hunched over a computer, poring over lists of the library's materials, trying to track down errant books?

If so, you're behind the times—and you may be missing exciting developments in the field. The fundamental nature of technical services has changed over the past several decades. The emphasis is no longer on performing traditional tasks such as cataloging or ordering materials. Now technical services librarians manage these processes, whether they are done by paraprofessionals or outsourced to vendors.

So what does this new field look like, and which librarians are best suited for it? The field appeals to those who are interested in complex systems, enjoy working with people, and have some aptitude with computers. They enjoy exploring new technology and how to apply it. They are versatile enough to catalog a few books in the morning, attend a budget meeting at lunch, train a new staff member in the afternoon, and finish up the day drafting procedures for acquiring and providing access to electronic resources. These individuals realize the growing importance of knowledge and do their best to provide access to it. Their skills and insights into the organization of knowledge are a vital part of the information environment.

This focus on innovation and flexibility is the hallmark of today's successful technical services librarians. Those interested in specializing in technical services need a solid knowledge of standard practices such as MARC formats, Library of Congress classification and subject headings, budgeting, accounting, and book trade practices. With this knowledge base, they should have the skills to juggle people, processes, and money, all with the goal of providing efficient access to materials.

Typical responsibilities for the technical services librarian include monitoring the complex web of processing tasks to determine the best ways to get projects done. These librarians also supervise staff members and lead teams, developing enthusiasm and encouraging new ideas and suggestions. Identifying jobs that should be outsourced is another crucial skill, as well as evaluating that outsourced work. Performing cost-benefit analyses or developing budgets for specific projects are routine tasks.

Of course, technical services librarians also must be well versed in library automation. This may include standard office automation, specialized library systems like OCLC, or particular integrated library systems. While knowledge of a particular system can be developed on the job, the new technical services librarian should have a good background in how library automated systems work and interact. For example, he or she should understand how the various modules (cataloging, acquisitions, circulation, and so on) work together and how changes can impact other parts of the system.

Along with this, such individuals need to have a broad understanding of library services and functions. They should be interested and involved in all areas of library work, including reference, bibliographic instruction, materials selection, and public service. They should also enjoy working with colleagues on library-wide projects such as designing and maintaining Web sites. This kind of "big picture" knowledge proves invaluable, because it allows them to help public services staff to plan and, ultimately, to understand the impact of technical processes on those who really matter—library users.

Index

ALA accredited MLS, importance of, 49–50, 141–142
Arrogance, need for in librarians, 127–130
Asheim, Lester, 124
Assessment, 4, 211

Bibliographic Instruction, 3, 26, 50, 78, 178, 188–189, 214–217
Bostwick, Arthur, 172
Business plans, 61–63, 131–132
Budgeting, 137
Behavior based interviewing, 132–133
Bridges, Karl, 151

California Lutheran University, 109–113
Catalogers, characteristics required of, 37–39, 227
Centers for Teaching Excellence, 213–217
Clarke, Arthur C., 169
Clarke, Edith Emily, 220–223

Collegiality, importance of, 30–31
Competition, importance for libraries, 157–159
Computer programming languages, usefulness for librarians, 69–70
Computers, 7, 8, 11, 26
Confidence, 43
Cornell University Library Digital Futures Plan, 63
Counseling skills, need for librarians to have, 59–60
Courage, 42
Creativity, 8, 14, 78
Critical thinking, 11
Curiosity, 8, 13–15, 74, 161
Customer service, role of in library services, 225–226
Cyberspace, 103, 178
Cynicism, 9

Darwin, Charles, 168
DeCandido, GraceAnne, 162
Dervin, Brenda, 95
Dewdney, Patricia, 95

Dewey, Melville, 210
Distance learners, 4
Dobb, Linda S., 211
Douglas, Gretchen, 214
Dunsire, Gordon, 17

Electronic resource librarians, 149–154
Emporia State University School of Library and Information Management, 94
Enthusiasm, 3, 41–42, 120

Faculty collaboration, 106
Faculty status, 86
Fargo, Lucille Foster, 171–172
Fine, Sarah, 60
Flexibility, 38, 42, 101–2, 120, 163, 180

Gorman, Michael, 105, 209
Grimes, Deborah, 215

Haricombe, Lorraine, 89
Helpfulness, importance of, 19, 57–58, 173–174,
Henry, John, 7
Hiring, 12–13
Hiring criteria, 14
Honesty, 19
Humor, 3, 43, 74, 165, 173

Information gap, 12
Information literacy, 33–35, 111, 179
Information specialists, as replacement for librarians, 110
Integrity, 19
Internet, 7, 11, 18, 22, 210
Interview, 21–23
Interview procedures, 111–113

Jargon, use by librarians, 130
Job advertisements, 66, 73, 97
Job candidates, characteristics of, 15, 18, 19, 22, 34–35, 46–47, 62–63, 65–66, 70–71, 74, 84, 90, 94–95, 98, 105, 115–117, 120–121, 129–130, 180–181, 206–7
Jordan, Barbara, 169

Karr, Alphonse, 93
Kellogg-ALISE Information Professions and Education Reform Project, 123
Kindness, 116
Knowledge management, role for librarians in, 147–148

Land grant universities, 1–4
Lasher, T.J., 89
Liberal arts education, 162
Librarians, public perception of, 119–120
Librarianship as midlife career, 139–143
Libraries, ancient history of, 18
Library automation, impact of, 145–146
Library profession, need for change, 53–55
Lipow, Anne Grodzins, 94
Listening skills, importance of, 60

Marketing, 43, 85–86,
McClintock, Barbara, 168
Mentoring, 3
Metz, Terry, 17
Misanthropy, 8
My Library, 69

Optimism, 41–42
Ortega y Gasset, José, 124–125
Osler, Sir William, 105
Outreach, 2
Outsourcing, 159

Pfleuger, Ken, 109
Positivism, 123–124
Pratt, Enoch, 209
Preservation, 153
Public libraries, 21–23
Public relations, 12, 137

Questia, 179

Reference interview, 29–30, 95, 117,
Roosevelt, Eleanor, 169
Ruschoff, Carlen, 151

Search committees, 132
Shills, Harold, 214
Special libraries, 171–174, 185
Stallings, Dees, 152
Stoffle, Carla, 17
Support staff, 31

Teams, 3
Technical services librarians, 227–228
Technology, importance of, 44,
    135–136
Tenaciousness, importance of, 117
Tennant, Roy, 179

Tolerance, 163
Tribal colleges, 2
Truman, Harry, 169

University of Arizona libraries,
    restructuring of, 81–82
University of Vermont, 219–223

Virtual learning, 1, 45
Virtual library, 11, 153, 193,
Virtual reference, 46, 178

Wu, D.Y., 150–151

About the Editor and Contributors

ABOUT THE EDITOR

KARL BRIDGES is Associate Professor, Information and Instruction Services, Bailey/Howe Library, University of Vermont.

THE CONTRIBUTORS

ROGER C. ADAMS, Kansas State University

CYNTHIA AKERS, Emporia State University

BETH AVERY, Western State College

MARIA C. BAGSHAW, Lake Erie College

JANE BIRKS, American University of Sharjah

COLLEEN BOFF, Bowling Green State University

RONALD N. BUKOFF, Centenary College of Louisiana

BARBARA BURD, Regent University

DAVID M. BYNOG, Rice University

FELIX T. CHU, Western Illinois University

JETTA CAROL CULPEPPER, Murray State University

MELINDA DERMODY, Saint Cloud State University

LEIGH ESTABROOK, University of Illinois at Urbana

KAREN FISCHER, Carleton College

MOLLY FLASPOHLER, Concordia College

KATHLEEN FLEMING, Wayne State University

JANET FOSTER, Danbury Public Library

RONDA GLIKIN, Eastern Michigan University

GWEN M. GREGORY, Colorado College

CHERYL GUNSELMAN, Washington State University

LESLIE M. HAAS, University of Utah

DANELLE HALL, Oklahoma City University

MARY ANNE HANSEN, Montana State University–Bozeman

SUSAN HERZOG, California Lutheran University

CRAIGHTON HIPPENHAMMER, Olivet Nazarene University

ALISON HOPKINS, Brantford Public Library

ANGELA K. HORNE, Cornell University

JENNIFER INGLIS, Piedmont College

MARIE JONES, East Tennessee State University

SHEILA KASPEREK, Mansfield University

VICKIE KLINE, York College of Pennsylvania

LIZ KOCEVAR-WEIDINGER, Longwood College

JANICE KRUEGER, University of the Pacific

NANCY KUHL, Yale University

ELEANOR L. LOMAX, Florida Atlantic University

BARBARA LOVATO-GASSMAN, Albuquerque Technical Vocational Institute

RANDALL M. MACDONALD, Florida Southern College

MARTHA HENN MCCORMICK, Indiana University–Purdue University Indianapolis

PATRICIA MORRIS, University of Arizona

MARY M. NOFSINGER, Washington State University

LORENA O'ENGLISH, Washington State University

JANET T. O'KEEFE, Flint Public Library

LIZ OESLEBY, Zayed University

NECIA PARKER-GIBSON, University of Arkansas–Fayetteville

ANDREW L. PEARSON, Florida Southern College

JOHN RIDDLE, Pennsylvania State University

MICHAEL J. ROSE, Northern Kentucky University

SHELLEY ROSS, University of Lethbridge

ANNE A. SALTER, Georgia Institute of Technology

BRIDGETTE SCOTT, Christian Brothers University

CAROL SINGER, Bowling Green State University

KENNETH A. SMITH, Valdosta State University

DAVID H. STANLEY, Seton Hill University

CARLA J. STOFFLE, University of Arizona

PHILIP SWAN, Hunter College

WENDY TAN, Hunter College

NINFA TREJO, University of Arizona

VIRGINIA E. YOUNG, Randolph Macon College